WRITERS AND THEIR WORK

ISOBEL ARMSTRONG
General Editor

BRYAN LOUGHREY
Advisory Editor

Romeo and Juliet

JULIET

What if it be a poison which the Friar
Subtly hath ministered to have me dead   4.3.23–4

An engraving by H. C. Selous illustrating Juliet's 'dismal scene' when she
takes the Friar's sleeping potion (4.3.14–59), from the popular *Cassell's
Illustrated Shakespeare* (1864–8) edited by one of the first woman editors of
Shakespeare, Mary Cowden Clarke. Selous portrays Juliet as a gothic
heroine, terrorized by thoughts of her dead male ancestors and her own
fear of death.

WWW

William Shakespeare

Romeo and Juliet

Sasha Roberts

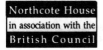

Northcote House
in association with the
British Council

First published in 1998 by Northcote House Publishers Ltd, Plymbridge House, Estover Road, Plymouth PL6 7PY, United Kingdom.
Tel: +44 (01752) 202368 Fax: +44 (01752) 202330.

British Library Cataloguing-in-Publication Data
A catalogue record for this book is available from the British Library

ISBN 0-7463-0812-4

Typeset by PDQ Typesetting, Newcastle-under-Lyme
Printed and bound in the United Kingdom

In memory of my grandmother,
Mary Kathleen Hull, 1897–1993

Contents

Illustrations

Acknowledgements

I would like to thank Bryan Loughrey for his editorial support, and Niky Rathbone and librarians at the Birmingham Shakespeare Library and Sylvia Morris and James Shaw at the Shakespeare Centre Library for their help with illustrations. For exchanging ideas about the play and this book, I would like to thank in particular Ann Thompson, Jason Scott-Warren, Ruth Roberts, and my students.

Illustration Acknowledgements

The Publishers gratefully acknowledge the following for supplying illustrations and granting permission for their use. Acknowledgements are listed according to figure numbers.

Cover detail and frontispiece: Shakespeare Centre Library, Stratford-upon-Avon; 1. Shakespeare Centre Library, Stratford-upon-Avon; 2. Shakespeare Centre Library: Joe Cocks Studio Collection; 3. Birmingham Shakespeare Library: Forrest Collection; 4. John Haynes/print courtesy of the Shakespeare Centre Library; 5. Birmingham Shakespeare Library: Forrest Collection; 6. Shakespeare Centre Library: Joe Cocks Studio Collection; 7. Birmingham Shakespeare Library: Forrest Collection; 8. Shakespeare Centre Library: Joe Cocks Studio Collection.

A Note on the Text

All references to *Romeo and Juliet* are to the New Cambridge edition, edited by G. Blakemore Evans, 1984, unless otherwise noted. References to the First Quarto (Q1) of *An Excellent Conceited Tragedie of Romeo and Juliet* are to Cedric Watt's edition for the series Shakespearean Originals: First Editions (Hemel Hempstead: Prentice Hall/Harvester Wheatsheaf, 1995). References to other Shakespeare plays are to *The Complete Works*, ed. Peter Alexander (London: Collins, 1970).

Cross references within this book are made to chapters, using the abbreviation Ch. Where applicable, page numbers following quotations refer to the reprint edition listed in the Select Bibliography.

Introduction

Romeo and Juliet is familiar to the point of cliché: widely taught at school and popularly performed, the play has become an icon of romantic love. It tells an apparently straightforward story of two lovers thwarted by parental opposition and a feuding society, and has long served as an introduction to Shakespeare. But the play has not always been held in high regard, and has been criticized as an immature, experimental work that fails to match the interest and complexity of Shakespeare's later tragedies (*Hamlet*, *Macbeth*, *Othello*, and *King Lear*). And, despite the interest in Shakespeare studies in issues of gender, domesticity, patriarchy, and the family (particularly since the 1980s), the play has not attracted as much critical attention as other Shakespeare plays from the 1590s, such as *A Midsummer Night's Dream* (*c*. 1594–5). It is as if *Romeo and Juliet* has been exhausted by overexposure. In my view, however, the play repays thorough investigation, for *Romeo and Juliet* is a complex and thought-provoking exploration of family relations, sexual desire, violence, and male bonding (amongst other issues). As Frank Kermode has argued, '*Romeo and Juliet* is not a simple play; to suppose that it is would be the most elementary mistake one could make concerning it' (p. 1057).

This book examines *Romeo and Juliet* in the light of recent critical thinking, sketching contexts, issues and debates of current interest in Shakespeare studies – especially around gender, sexuality, history, ritual, and textual transmission (that is, the different forms in which a text is reproduced). One of the most influential developments in Renaissance literary criticism of the 1980s and 1990s has been a concern with the relationship between literary texts and history. Because *Romeo and Juliet* engages with contemporary preoccupations in Elizabethan

1

England, this book considers some of the play's historical contexts. *Romeo and Juliet* is a multifaceted play that may be interpreted in many ways, but one reading of the play has tended to dominate criticism and performance: the view that *Romeo and Juliet* represents an ideal of, or idealizes, romantic love. To be sure, *Romeo and Juliet* is a love-story; however, engaging with the Elizabethan cultural contexts of *Romeo and Juliet* can also release a refreshing scepticism over Romeo and Juliet as romantic heroes and their love as an ideal. The play has also been reworked, indeed reinvented, over a period of four centuries, and this book also addresses nineteenth- and twentieth-century criticism and performance of the play (especially recent work). Chapter 1 questions the textual 'stability' of *Romeo and Juliet* by considering the 'rival' texts of the play published in 1597 and 1599 and the alternative readings they offer, the censorship of the play (which still persists today), and the alteration and adaptation of the play in performance. Chapter 2 examines Shakespeare's complex portrayal of family relations in the light of early modern cultural practice, focusing upon adolescence and maturity, clandestine marriage, the characterization of Romeo and Juliet as melancholics, patriarchal and matriarchal authority, and the Capulets' marital relations. In Chapter 3 I consider different aspects of the construction of identity in *Romeo and Juliet*, beginning with distinctions between public and private domains in the play and the politics of space and subjectivity they reveal, and the play's extraordinary imagery of the grotesque and maternal body. I then turn to the fashioning of femininity and sexuality (with a focus on Juliet) and effeminacy (with a focus on Romeo), and examine different codes of masculinity in the play, male bonding, and the possibilities for 'homoerotic' readings of the play. The chapter concludes by considering distinctions of class and community with a focus on the Nurse's social status and historical practices of wet-nursing, and on the Friar's infiltration of the 'secular' community and his possible evocation of anti-Catholic prejudice. Chapter 4 examines Petrarchism and bawdy talk as discourses in dialogue with each other, complementing and undermining the idealization of romantic love in the play, and considers the ritual significance of key motifs in the play: betrothal, bridal beds, and deathbeds.

2

This book does not pretend to be comprehensive – rather, I have focused upon questions that have particularly intrigued me about the play, in the hope of opening up debates that readers will pursue or contest for themselves. What has surprised me, in returning to *Romeo and Juliet*, is the play's complexity. Looking beyond *Romeo and Juliet* as an icon of romantic love or an easy introduction to Shakespeare reveals a work that is multidimensional, ambivalent, and conflicted; a play that subtly explores the fascinating mess of human relations.

1

Which *Romeo and Juliet?*

To begin with an unsettling thought: despite appearances, there is no definitive text of Shakespeare's *Romeo and Juliet*. This is because several versions of the play have survived from Shakespeare's lifetime – distinct publications with different texts that allow for alternative interpretations of the play – and we do not know which version, if any, Shakespeare actually authorized (his name does not even appear upon Elizabethan editions of the play). Moreover, the Elizabethan texts of *Romeo and Juliet* have undergone considerable adaptation and emendment in the play's long publication and performance history. *Romeo and Juliet* has long been viewed as an (overly) familiar, stable, and secure entity, but in fact the play exists in many different versions – both textual and theatrical. In order to recover the play's complexity we need to be aware of the differences between editions as well as those between text and production, and of the interpretive hand of both the editor and the producer of the play.

Until the mid-nineteenth century popular editions and productions of the play were based upon David Garrick's 1748 adaptation of *Romeo and Juliet*, which sought 'to clear the Original as much as possible, from the Jingle and Quibble which were always thought a great Objection to performing it'. Garrick omitted Romeo's first love for Rosaline, considered 'a Blemish in his Character'; Juliet's age was raised from 13 to 18, thereby avoiding worries about her precocious sexuality; bawdy quibbles were ruthlessly cut from the play in the interests of modesty; whole scenes were added to the play, including a funeral procession at the beginning of act five and a sentimental exchange in the final scene between Romeo and Juliet, who was allowed to wake up just before Romeo dies; finally, Garrick

4

concluded the play with a definitive moral: 'From private feuds, what dire misfortunes flow;/Whate'er the cause, the sure effect is WOE'.[1] It was not until 1845 that the Shakespearean text was revived (though still in censored form) by the American actress Charlotte Cushman – who played the part of Romeo opposite her sister Susan's Juliet, inspiring a run of female Romeos (see. Ch. 3 and fig. 1).

Adaptation, emendment, sentimentalization, and sanitation are still features of modern productions and, more surprisingly perhaps, editions of the play. Zeffirelli's film of 1968, for instance, cuts almost two-thirds of the play, changes lines, adds whole scenes (such as Juliet's funeral procession), and in so doing 'altered the very fabric of the play's style'.[2] Similarly, Luhrmann's 1996 film makes significant cuts and alterations, particularly to the female characters (for instance Juliet's 'bedding ballad' or epithalamion, 3.2.1–31, was reduced to only a few lines). Michael Bogdanov's 1986 production for the RSC, set in modern Italy, cut the final scene altogether after Juliet's death and concluded the play with a publicity stunt posing as a press conference: the feuding families grouped to have their pictures taken by the *paparazzi*, the gold statues were unveiled in front of the cameras, and the Prince was hounded by the media. In a sense Bogdanov, like Garrick, framed the play with a moral – in this case the greed and cynicism of bourgeois culture and the media. The 'sanitation' of the Shakespearean text is still ongoing in the twentieth century: Zeffirelli's film omitted many of the play's bawdy jokes, while five leading American high-school editions published in the late 1980s and enforced in some states ruthlessly censored the play's sexual innuendo – even emending the Nurse's anecdote on breastfeeding.[3] As recently as 1989 Hugh M. Richmond argued that many productions persist in the 'sentimental misreading' of *Romeo and Juliet*, particularly in the presentation of Romeo and Juliet as tragic heroes rather than misguided adolescents (pp. 224–5). The end product becomes a sanitized and sentimentalized play that is a far cry from the boisterous, sceptical, bawdy, and sometimes brutal versions of the play published in Elizabethan England.

Romeo and Juliet was first published in cheap, paperback form in 1597 as 'AN/EXCELLENT/conceited Tragedie/OF/Romeo and Juliet,/As it hath been often (with great applause)/plaid

1   Charlotte Cushman as Romeo, *c.* 1845. Charlotte played the part of
Romeo to great acclaim opposite her sister Susan's Juliet and was
responsible for restoring Shakespeare's text (heavily cut) to the stage,
breaking the hold of Garrick's version of the play. She sought to
emphasize Romeo's vigour and masculinity: 'Miss Cushman is a very
dangerous young man,' noted one observer (Joseph Leach, *Bright
Particular Star*, 1970, p. 175).

publiquely, by the right Ho-/nourable the L[ord] of *Hunsdon* /his Servants', a volume known as the First Quarto or Q1 (a quarto volume was a small, inexpensive book made up of four-leaf units of paper). Two years later in 1599 appeared the Second Quarto or Q2: 'THE/MOST EX-/cellent and lamentable/Tragedie, of Romeo/and *Juliet./Newly corrected, augmented, and/amended:/* As it hath bene sundry times publiquely acted, by the/right Honourable the Lord Chamberlaine/his Servants'. Notice that while the title of the First Quarto draws attention to the play's ingenuity ('conceited' denoted intelligence, wit, and conception in the period), the Second Quarto title points to the pitiful, 'lamentable' ends of the protagonists. (Two further quartos, Q3 and Q4, followed in 1609 and 1622, and they in turn formed the basis of another version of the play in the posthumous, collected works of Shakespeare of 1623, known as the First Folio). These 'rival' texts of *Romeo and Juliet* ought to be of concern to readers, students, actors, producers, and audiences of *Romeo and Juliet* because they allow for alternative readings of the play.

The differences between the texts of Q1 and Q2 are considerable: Q2 is some 800 lines longer than Q1 and there are numerous 'textual variants' (differing words or phrases) between the two editions.[4] What interests me about these variants is the alternative interpretations of the play they have to offer. One of the most striking differences between the texts is that Q1 does not include the Chorus ('Now old desire doth in his death-bed lie', 1.5.144–57), which in Q2 can serve to cast doubt upon the romantic integrity of the young lovers' 'passion' (1.5.156; see Ch. 4). Similarly, the opening prologue of Q1 omits the sacrificial theme often argued to be central to the play's interpretation: that Romeo and Juliet 'with their death bury their parents' strife' (Q2, Prologue, 8–11). Thus Q1 does not establish any expectation that the lovers are destined to be sacrificial lambs, paying with their lives to bring about peace. The opening scene of Q1 also omits the quarrel between Benvolio and Tybalt, so Tybalt is not introduced as a man consumed by hate ('peace? I hate the word,/As I hate hell, all Montagues, and thee' appears only in Q2, 1.1.61–2); Capulet and Montague do not intervene in the fight, so Capulet is not the aggressor he appears, if sometimes comically, in Q2, and Lady Capulet and Lady Montague do not contest their husbands ('why call you for a sword?', 'Thou shalt not stir no foot to seek a foe' only appear in Q2, 1.1.67 and 71). Similarly in 1.3, as Steven Urkowitz points out, Q2 presents Lady Capulet 'as a hard-driving advocate for Paris', while in Q1 she seems far more gentle, 'delicately introducing the topic of marriage to her daughter' (p. 298; see Ch. 2). The final scene of Q1 makes explicit the Friar's disapproval of Capulet's behaviour – 'her Father sought by *foule constraint*/To marrie her to Paris' (Q1, p. 97; emphasis added) – while in Q2 the Friar reports less controversially that Capulet arranged the marriage out of apparently good intentions, 'to remove that siege of grief from her' (5.3.236–7). Or consider the issue of naming in the play: in Q1 'Montague' is consistently printed as 'Mountague' – a name which carries connotations of venereal disease ('ague' means disease or fever, while 'to mount' was slang for a man's posture during sexual intercourse; see p. 39 on images of venereal disease in the play).

Editors, however, have traditionally been more interested in Q1's distinctive stage directions, which are fuller and more precise than those in Q2 and are often adopted by modern editors. Q1, for instance, specifies domestic and ritual details that are absent in Q2 – such as the stage direction 'all but the Nurse goe foorth, casting Rosemary on her and shutting the Curtens' of Juliet's supposed deathbed (p. 87). More importantly, Q1 stage directions hint at characters' behaviour: in the scene before Romeo and Juliet's marriage, for instance, Q1 instructs 'Enter Juliet somewhat fast, and embraceth Romeo' (p. 61). The stage direction emphasizes Juliet's sensual passion and hurry to be married, evoking the impatience the Friar has just warned Romeo against: 'love moderately, long love doth so;/Too swift arrives as tardy as too slow' (2.6.14–15). Similarly, when Romeo threatens to kill himself in Friar Lawrence's cell, the Q1 stage direction reads 'He offers to stab himselfe, and Nurse snatches the dagger away' (p. 71). There is no equivalent stage direction in Q2 and the scene is usually played with the Friar struggling to disarm Romeo – but Q1's stage direction hints that despite the Friar's maxims of wisdom he is not adept in practical emergencies; the Nurse is quicker-thinking.

The 'rival' texts of *Romeo and Juliet* present editors with the problem of which text to publish in modern editions of the play:

generally editors have ignored Q3, Q4, the First Folio, and much of Q1, and base their editions on Q2 of 1599 – inserting act and scene divisions, making corrections to what they consider to be misprints in Q2, and incorporating stage directions or textual variants from Q1 that they consider appropriate. Consequently, a modern edition of *Romeo and Juliet* is a mediated text, already filtered through an editor's judgement. Editors base their texts on Q2 because it is traditionally regarded as a 'Good Quarto', an authoritative text that derives from Shakespeare's (lost) original manuscript of the play, while Q1 is deemed a 'Bad Quarto', an unreliable and unauthoritative text. How do editors arrive at this judgement?

First, a brief background to the publication of Shakespeare's plays: apart from his highly successful narrative poems (*Venus and Adonis*, 1593, and *Lucrece*, 1594), Shakespeare did not write for publication: his plays were written for and belonged to the acting companies he worked with (hence Q1 and Q2 of *Romeo and Juliet* do not even bear Shakespeare's name). After completion of the manuscript (or 'foul papers'), a single copy of the play was neatly written out in full (known as the 'fair copy') and sent for approval by the Master of the Revels (the state censor). The acting company might then use the 'fair copy' as their single, legible complete copy of the play; actors generally had only their individual lines and cues written out for them. There was no law of copyright as such, and this allowed for the production of 'pirate' versions of popular plays by actors (or possibly members of an audience), who wrote out the play from memory and then sold it at a profit to a publisher. Q1 *Romeo and Juliet* has traditionally been regarded as an unreliable 'pirate' edition, and in 1948 H. R. Hoppe proposed that the actors playing Romeo and Paris were the most likely piratical 'reporters' as it is their lines which most closely correspond to the Q2 text.[5] Once a 'pirate' edition was in the public domain the only way for an acting company to counter it was to produce an 'authorized' edition of their own, based either on the author's 'foul papers' or the 'fair copy' of the play: the 'newly corrected, augmented, and amended' edition of Q2 *Romeo and Juliet* is generally considered to be an authorized edition. More recently, some critics and editors have argued that Q2 represents Shakespeare's careful revision of the play; a final draft, so to speak. In 1994, for instance, E. Pearlman argued that in Q2 Shakespeare 'can be found perfecting a line or phrase, re-thinking the architecture of the whole, and even importing into the play incidents that are extrinsic to its initial design' (p. 316).

But there are good reasons for reading and performing the Q1 text of *Romeo and Juliet*. In the first place, Q1's textual variants yield alternative readings of *Romeo and Juliet*, opening up new possibilities for interpretation and debate in the critical analysis and performance of the play. Secondly, if we want to consider *Romeo and Juliet* in terms of its performance in the 1590s then Q1 – with its full and precise stage directions, and omissions which whittle the play down to the proposed 'two howres traffique of our Stage' (Q2 takes longer to perform) – seems to represent a performance-text, allowing more insight into contemporary stage practice than the text of Q2. Recent critical thinking has emphasized Shakespeare's plays as part of a theatrical rather than a literary tradition: as Graham Holderness argues, 'the variations between the texts that have come down to us reflect the conditions of a theatre in which the essence of drama was not literature, but performance, not a written or printed but an oral medium of communication'.[6] Thirdly, the notion that Shakespeare's texts can be ranked as 'good' or 'bad' (in which the 'good', 'authoritative' text reputedly brings us closer to what Shakespeare 'originally' intended) has increasingly been questioned: 'bad' quartos, as Leah Marcus argues, have come to be regarded 'as different rather than debased'.[7] Finally, we should remember the early reception of Shakespeare's texts as reading matter for late-sixteenth and early-seventeenth-century readers: early modern readers of *Romeo and Juliet* were as likely to own or read an 'unauthorized' version of Shakespeare's play as they were to consult the 'newly corrected' Q2. For the first time in decades Q1 *Romeo and Juliet* is now widely available in paperback in Cedric Watts's 1995 edition for the controversial *Shakespearean Originals: First Editions* series; perhaps we can look forward to more critical engagement with and performance of this often-ignored text of the play.

2

Family Dynamics

Criticism of *Romeo and Juliet* has often centred upon what *type* of tragedy the play is: a tragedy of character, in which Romeo and Juliet are tragically 'flawed' and responsible for their own deaths, or a tragedy of fate, whereby Romeo and Juliet are victims of a feuding society.[1] Some have questioned whether the play can properly be called a tragedy at all: James Calderwood, for instance, argues that Romeo and Juliet are 'insufficiently endowed with complexity' to become tragic heroes: 'they become a study of victimage and sacrifice, not tragedy' (p. 101). In addition, the dependency of the play's outcome upon a series of evasions and accidents (culminating in Friar John's failure to deliver Friar Lawrence's letter to Romeo) is seen to diminish, if not undermine, the tragic impetus of the play.[2] Thus for H. B. Charlton, *Romeo and Juliet* represents an 'unsuccessful experiment'; an 'apprentice piece' that shows the marks of Shakespeare's immaturity as a dramatist (p. 59). Other critics, such as Susan Snyder, have stressed instead the play's deliberate and radical mix of comic and tragic genres – a mix recognized by Robert Burton in 1621 when he described the play as a 'Tragicomedy of love'.[3] *Romeo and Juliet* starts out with many conventions from romantic and Roman comedy, such as the resourceful heroine pitted against parental opposition, or the stock figure of the bawd evoked by the Nurse. The play's gravity is repeatedly undercut by humour, opening with a boisterous, bawdy exchange between Sampson and Gregory (1.1.1–29) which counters the serious tone of the Prologue. Only after the death of Mercutio in 3.1 (usually described as the 'turning point' in the play) does *Romeo and Juliet* begin to behave more like a tragedy. For an Elizabethan audience accustomed to more uniformity in dramatic styles (think of the more

11

conventional gravity of opening scenes in Shakespeare's other tragedies), *Romeo and Juliet* may have disrupted audience expectations of tragic form, mood, and decorum – and in so doing called into question the limits and limitations of genre.[4]

In my view, however, the most interesting questions around the play's genre lie in its bold choice of subject matter. Today the death of young lovers seems a natural (or, more precisely, naturalized) choice for a tragedy, but in 1594–6, when the play was probably written, tragedy typically focused upon the fall of political figures such as kings, princes, or generals (consider Shakespeare's more conventional tragic heroes: Hamlet, Othello, King Lear, Macbeth). As Harry Levin notes, Shakespeare's contemporaries:

> would have been surprised, and possibly shocked, at seeing lovers taken so seriously. Legend, it had been heretofore taken for granted, was the proper matter for serious drama; romance was the stuff of the comic stage. (p. 45)

Shakespeare effectively invites the audience to consider adolescent passion and parent–child relations as the stuff of serious drama. Furthermore, the play allows for considerable complexity in the depiction of marital, patriarchal, matriarchal, and filial relations, and engages with contemporary concerns about the nature of power and its abuse within the family. The fact that *Romeo and Juliet* has been co-opted as a 'universal' love-story that transcends time and cultural difference should not blind us to the topical relevance of the play in the late-sixteenth century. Rather, by addressing the historical context of family relations in early modern England we become more attuned to the complexities and contradictions at work in Shakespeare's portrayal of a family in crisis.

ADOLESCENCE AND MARRIAGE

Romeo and Juliet has long been regarded as a play that speaks to the young: 'young people throughout the entire world,' writes Julia Kristeva, 'whatever their race, religion, or social status, identify with the adolescents of Verona' (p. 298). In turn, the play has often been viewed as a validation of the younger generation against the older, affirming the rights of children to choose their own marriage partners.[5] But, as Susan Bassnett argued in 1993, although twentieth-century directors have sought to make Romeo and Juliet 'accessible by stressing their relevance to contemporary teenagers at odds with their parents, this grossly oversimplifies matters. The younger generation is not straightforwardly heroic or admirable in contrast to narrow-minded elders. Each generation has its faults' (p. 66). In this section I investigate the play's portrayal of romantic love and marriage among teenagers by turning to historical practices of marriage and 'adolescence' in early modern England, and sketching Romeo and Juliet's presentation as 'love-melancholics'.

It has become a commonplace in criticism and performance that Shakespeare's *Romeo and Juliet* represents an ideal – and an endorsement – of romantic love. The feminist critic Dympna Callaghan has interestingly elaborated on this view by arguing that *Romeo and Juliet* promotes the *ideology* of romantic love by validating Romeo and Juliet's marriage. In so doing, the play makes marriage and the nuclear family 'the social destination of desire' (p. 88). In effect, the play endorses the 'bourgeois family form' advocated by early modern Protestant treatises on marriage, and thus serves the needs of 'an emergent social order' which looked to 'a new conception of the family as an independent economic unit within a market economy' (pp. 62 and 65). But in my view *Romeo and Juliet* is less mechanistic and more ambivalent in its presentation of desire than Callaghan suggests, for the play questions Romeo and Juliet's love-affair and marriage as an 'ideal'. Not only is Juliet shown to be an exceptionally young bride, but Romeo and Juliet's marriage is clandestine; they are both guilty of disobedience to their parents and the maturity of their actions is doubted. The play *complicates* rather than validates passion and clandestine marriage among teenagers. This is not to deny that Romeo and Juliet engage in romance, nor that the play dwells upon discourses and experiences of romantic love. Rather, my point is to consider and question the emphasis placed upon the element of romance, especially an *idealized* romance, in many interpretations of the play – for notions of romantic love provide only one of several contexts in which to read Romeo and Juliet's relationship.

Shakespeare's *Romeo and Juliet* centres upon a 13-year-old girl marrying (and then having sex with) her teenage lover of one day's standing. Shakespeare deliberately sought to emphasize Juliet's youth: he altered his principal source for the play, Arthur Brooke's *Tragicall Historye of Romeus and Juliet* (1562), by lowering Juliet's age from 16 to 13, and her young age is stressed on several occasions: 'My child is yet a stranger in the world,/She hath not seen the change of fourteen years' (1.2.8–9), 'She's not fourteen' (repeated twice, 1.3.13, 1.3.15), 'On Lammas-eve at night shall she be fourteen' (1.3.22). Shakespeare's Juliet is an exceptionally young bride for the period. In early modern England the single most important event for young people in the transition to adulthood was marriage, and most men and women only married once they had achieved some measure of economic stability and independence, usually in their late twenties for men and early twenties for women. Even among the aristocracy where age at marriage was often lower, it was extremely rare for a couple to embark on married life together until they were nearly 20: in the early seventeenth century, for instance, the Countess of Warwick's brother who had married in his late teens was sent to France 'being then judged to be too young to live with his wife'; similarly her own son, who married at the age of 19, was sent abroad as the couple were considered 'too young to live together'.[6] *Romeo and Juliet*, far from naturalizing Juliet's age at marriage, deliberately provokes questions of propriety. Indeed, for eighteenth- and nine-teenth-century producers and critics of the play Juliet's age at marriage posed a problem of decency: Garrick sought to make the marriage more respectable by increasing Juliet's age to 18, while Mrs Elliott argued in 1885 that 'to represent Juliet on our stage as of the age Shakespeare makes her would be odious and absurd. It would be ridiculous to the British public to see a mere child in years so precocious in feeling and understanding' (p. 178). Certainly 'the British public' continue to be sceptical about love and marriage for a 13-year-old girl: in 1996 Sarah Cooke, the 13-year-old 'child bride' of an 18-year-old Turk, was criticized for her hopeless naïvety in believing she had found true love, and her parents were roundly attacked for allowing their daughter to marry so young ('You must have been mad, Mum', read the editorial headline in the *Sun* on Monday, 22 January 1996).

But Romeo and Juliet's marriage is also controversial because it is clandestine: covert, secret, furtive, unauthorized, illicit. In

Shakespeare's principal source of the play, Brooke's *Romeus*, the keynote of the lovers' marriage is not romantic love, but controversy, scandal, and shame:

> to this ende (good Reader) is this tragicall matter written, to describe unto thee a coople of unfortunate lovers, thralling themselves to unhonest desire, neglecting the authoritie and advise of parents and frendes, conferring their principall counsels with dronken gossypes, and superstitious friers (the naturally fitte instruments of unchastitie) attemptyng all adventures of perull, for thattanyng of their wished lust, usyng auriculer confession (the key of whoredome, and treason) for furtherance of theyr purpose, *abusyng the honorable name of lawefull mariage, to cloke the shame of stolne contractes*, finally, by all meanes of unhonest lyfe, hastyng to most unhappye deathe.[7]

For Brooke, Romeo and Juliet have only themselves to blame for their deaths: their marriage is a transgressive act that violates social convention – a shameful stolen contract that dishonours 'lawefull mariage'. It was not until Hardwicke's Marriage Act of 1754 that the procedure for marriage was formalized in England, and for the Elizabethan elite marriage was marked by a protracted series of public rituals and social transactions – generally encompassing betrothal (a formal commitment to marry), negotiations over the bride's dowry, a public announcement of the intended marriage in church on three separate occasions (usually known as 'reading the banns'), a publicly witnessed wedding, church blessing, family celebrations and, finally, the bedding ceremony in which the marriage was consummated (see Ch. 4). Although Romeo and Juliet's marriage is in theory legally binding, it disregards socially accepted practice; it operates, as Julia Kristeva notes, outside the 'law' of custom (p. 298). Hence the Friar's anxious opening request that the heavens 'chide us not' (2.6.2) at Romeo and Juliet's marriage, and Juliet's misgivings that the Friar 'should be *dishonoured*' by secretly marrying her to Romeo (4.3.26, emphasis added). It seems unlikely, then, that an Elizabethan audience would respond to Romeo and Juliet's marriage as an ideal. Indeed, up until the twentieth century the play was used didactically to illustrate the consequences of bad behaviour: in 1775 Mrs Griffith described Romeo and Juliet's catastrophic deaths as 'poetic justice, for their having ventured upon an unweighed engagement together, without the concurrence and consent of their parents' (p. 497); similarly *The Young Lady's Library* of 1829 argued that the play was 'a most lamentable illustration of the misery which results from the unbridled indulgence of bad passions' (p. 17), while the *Westminster Review* of 1845 reported that 'prudent matrons of rank have taken their girls to witness the performance of this play, as a warning against the dangers attendant on a clandestine union' (p. 4).

By disobeying her parents Juliet disregards orthodox ideology (that is, the 'official' or 'dominant' way of viewing the world) in early modern England, which called for the obedience of children: as William Perkins put it in 1609, 'the authority of parents must not be resisted or violated'.[8] The historian Lawrence Stone has argued that the early modern elite 'successfully internalized' filial obedience and that parental authority extended to choosing a child's marriage partner (p. 130). Thus:

> To an Elizabethan audience the tragedy of Romeo and Juliet, like that of Othello, lay not so much in their ill-starred romance as in the way they brought destruction upon themselves by violating the norms of the society in which they lived, which in the former case meant strict filial obedience and loyalty to the traditional friendships and enemies of the lineage. An Elizabethan courtier would be familiar enough with the bewitching passion of love to feel some sympathy with the young couple, but he would see clearly enough where duty lay. (p. 70)

Stone's 'contextual' reading of *Romeo and Juliet* echoes Brooke's moralistic interpretation of the story. In fact the historical realities of parental authority over a daughter's marriage were more complex and locally variable than Stone's account suggests, and as Keith Wrightson has since argued parental matchmaking 'was not uniform even at the highest social levels.... even for the children of the social elite, marital initiative did not lie solely in the hands of parents', and children retained by law the power of veto over who they were to marry (pp. 73 and 79). While social and economic factors influenced the choice of marriage partner among the elite, 'the ideal match was rarely conceived of solely in terms of economic gain, but comprehended a range of desirable traits and was not uninfluenced by romantic expectations fuelled by the romantic literature of the day' (p. 80). Wrightson cites the case of Bridget

Oglander, who in 1649 sought to marry a young gentleman whom her father disapproved of: 'upon "her importunity" and her declared resolve "to have him whatsoever became of her", he gave way and consented to the match' (p. 73). Consensus was the keynote of most marriage negotiations in the period. Shakespeare's *Romeo and Juliet* thus examines not a typical but an exceptional marriage, in which consensus is replaced by deceit and division (with Juliet keeping her marriage plans secret from her parents) and extreme parental pressure is imposed by Capulet.

Further doubt is cast upon Romeo and Juliet's marriage in terms of their characterization as adolescents, not adults. 'Adolescence' (or, to use a less anachronistic term, youth) was commonly associated in the period with rashness, disobedience, lust, and a dangerous indulgence in romance. In her study of *Adolescence and Youth in Early Modern England* (1994), Ilana Krausman Ben-Amos argues that young people were commonly depicted 'as singularly attached to the "pleasure of this bodye", to the "voluptye and carnal desires of this bodye", and youth was described as a period in which indulgence in carnal lust, lasciviousness and sensual delights reigned' (p. 12). She observes that spiritual biographers remembered adolescence as a period of illicit sexual activity: John Bunyan, for instance, noted that in his teenage years 'I did still let loose the reins to my lust, and delighted in all transgression against God'.[9] In popular literature desire was commonly associated with youth: ballads and chapbooks portraying courtship and sexual relations overwhelmingly focus upon young and unmarried (as opposed to adult or married) lovers. Romantic literature was often characterized as frivolous and associated with young women readers: Mary Rich, the Countess of Warwick, recalled how 'vain and foolish' she was at the age of 14 because of the time she wasted 'seeing and reading plays and romances'.[10] Adolescents were seen, and later saw themselves, as particularly vulnerable to lust, rashness, and a predilection for romance.

Romeo and Juliet's indulgence in romance and their impatience not simply to marry but to consummate their marriage (have sex) could thus have evoked stereotypes of youthful lust, rashness, and folly to an Elizabethan audience. Indeed, the play repeatedly draws attention to the young couple's rashness and impetuosity: 'It is too rash, too unadvised, too sudden', says Juliet of their 'contract' (2.2.118); 'they stumble that run fast' (Friar Lawrence, 2.3.94); 'violent delights have violent ends.... Therefore love moderately' (Friar Lawrence, 2.6.9–14). Indeed the Prologue alerts the audience to Romeo and Juliet's 'misadventured piteous overthrows' (l. 7). The figure of Rosaline can play an important role in the characterization of Romeo as an impatient, lusty lover: switching his attention from one woman to another within a matter of hours, Romeo is arguably fickle and rash (alternatively, he has reached a more mature love; see Ch. 4). The ghost of Romeo's love for Rosaline haunts how we view his love for Juliet. Ostensibly offering a non-partisan, 'objective' overview of the play, the Chorus describes Romeo's feelings for Juliet not in terms of true love, but as an 'affection' that substitutes an 'old desire' (Romeo's love for Rosaline); a desire, moreover, that is strongly inflected by sexual appetite ('Now old desire doth in his death-bed lie,/ And young affection gapes to be his heir', 2.1.143–4; see Ch. 4 on the use of bawdy in the Chorus). The young couple are described as 'bewitched' (1.5.149) – a word often used in the period to evoke a naïve or uncontrolled submission to devious or suspicious behaviour. As John F. Andrews suggests, there is nothing 'to suggest that the Chorus considers what Romeo feels for Juliet to be superior in kind to what he felt for Rosaline',[11] while Blakemore Evans finds the Chorus 'unsympathetic (almost moralistic) towards the lovers' (p. 88). Garrick omitted Romeo's love for Rosaline on the grounds that it was a 'Blemish' in Romeo's character; so too did Zeffirelli, and in effect both producers idealized Romeo and Juliet's romance and sentimentalized the play (see also Ch. 1).

Romeo and Juliet's rapid maturity has frequently been emphasized in criticism and performance, often in order to recuperate their actions as heroic (see for instance Cusack, Garber, Kahn, and O'Brien). Romeo is argued to manifest 'a new awareness and determination' when he gets the news of Juliet's supposed death in Mantua,[12] while 'in the short space of four days [Juliet] lives a life of many years. She appears before us a child, she leaves us a woman'.[13] But I would question how far such a transformation actually takes place, for in my view the text(s) point instead to Romeo and Juliet's continued rashness, lack of control, and immaturity. In the final scene Romeo speaks of his 'savage-wild' intentions 'More fierce and more inexorable far/Than empty tigers or the roaring sea', threatens to tear Balthasar 'joint by joint' (5.3.35–9), and describes himself to Paris as a 'madman' (5.3.67) – hardly a picture of controlled maturity. Friar Lawrence describes Juliet's first proposal of suicide as 'desperate' (4.1.69), and in the final scene explains that Juliet was 'too desperate' to leave the tomb, and in this state of mind 'did violence on herself' (5.3.263–4): again, he stresses her lack of control.[14]

Ben-Amos characterizes adolescence and youth in early modern English society, as 'a long and dynamic phase in the life cycle – a phase which consisted of a series of mental, social and economic processes through which the young were transformed into adults', and which might easily last up to fifteen years or more (pp. 8 and 11). *Romeo and Juliet*, in my view, does not telescope this transformation into four days; Romeo and Juliet never secure the economic independence or social recognition of adulthood (indeed, they never address the social or economic practicalities or consequences of their future lives), and by rushing headlong into marriage and then committing suicide Romeo and Juliet do not so much mature as play out the 'misadventured piteous overthrows' ascribed to them in the opening prologue (Prologue, l. 7). For most early modern commentators suicide was a desperate, violent act that ran against God's will (consider Hamlet's qualms over suicide, and the argument over whether Ophelia should be buried in consecrated ground); less an act of stoicism than a critical failure of faith. Significantly, one of Shakespeare's contemporaries, Robert Burton, was sceptical about Romeo and Juliet's behaviour: quoting from Shakespeare's play, he used the young lovers as an example of violent excess. In *The Anatomy of Melancholy* (1621) Burton described the pitiful symptoms of those who love unwisely in the extremity of passion: the love-melancholic. From excessive love 'comes Repentance, Dotage, they lose themselves, their wits, and make shipwreck of their fortunes altogether: madness, to make away themselves and others, violent death.' To prove his point Burton quotes from the concluding couplet of Shakespeare's *Romeo and Juliet*: 'Who ever heard a story of more woe,/Than that of Juliet and Romeo?'[15]

This does not preclude sympathy for Romeo and Juliet and their plight; rather, it calls for caution in the romanticization of Romeo and Juliet, a romanticization that is partly enabled by suppressing the fact of their teenage years.

Burton's allusion to Romeo and Juliet in the context of an analysis of melancholia is revealing, for it alerts us to their characterization as love-melancholics. And by portraying both Romeo and Juliet as suffering from melancholia, the play signals their emotional instability. Rejected by Rosaline, Romeo is initially distinguished by his 'sorrows', 'sadness', and isolation (1.1.145 and 154). Shunning the company of others and stealing 'into the covert of the wood' (1.1.116), he exhibits the symptoms Robert Burton observed of the male love-melancholic in *The Anatomy of Melancholy* – that they 'delight in floods and waters, desert[ed] places, to walk alone in orchards, gardens, private walks, back lanes; averse from company' (1.3.1(2), vol. 3, p. 396). As Helen Hackett has recently argued, the sorrowful, tearful, reclusive lover suffering from 'melancholy' appears in early modern culture as a 'predominantly masculine' type.[16] Burton does, however, include in *The Anatomy of Melancholy* a section on 'Symptoms of Maids', 'Nuns', and 'Widow's Melancholy' – a classification which, as Hackett points out, 'immediately associates female melancholy with lack of sex'. Whereas male love-melancholics should be persuaded out of their passion by their friends and family – rather as Montague, Benvolio, Mercutio, and Friar Lawrence seek to 'counsel' Romeo (1.1.133) – Burton advises that for female melancholics 'the best and surest remedy of all, is to see them well placed, and married to good husbands' (1.3.2(4), vol. 3, p. 416). This is precisely the 'remedy' applied to the 'evermore weeping' Juliet (3.5.69). Lady Capulet announces to Juliet that her 'careful father', 'to put thee from thy heaviness,/Hath sorted out a sudden day of joy' (3.5.108–9); as Paris later explains, 'her father counts it dangerous/ That she do give her sorrow so much sway;/And in his wisdom hastes our marriage/To stop the inundation of her tears' (4.1.9–12). The sense that marriage is the appropriate 'cure' (1.1.146) for Juliet's depression is made more explicit still in Shakespeare's primary source for the play, Brooke's *Romeus*, in which 'Capilet' endeavours 'to procure/A husband for our daughter yong,/her sickness faynt to cure'.[17] Thus while Romeo's melancholy is treated as intellectual or emotional suffering, Juliet's melancholy is attributed to her lack of a husband: Capulet, Lady Capulet, Paris, Montague, and Benvolio respond to Romeo and Juliet according to gendered notions of the cause and treatment of melancholia. And for an early modern audience the presence of their melancholy indicates, in turn, Romeo and Juliet's depression, emotional instability and lack of maturity.

MOTHERS AND FATHERS

Issues of power and control, obedience and disobedience, are central to *Romeo and Juliet*. Feminist critics of *Romeo and Juliet* have stressed the crucial role of patriarchal power in the play: 'rebellion against parental authority', argued Susan Bassnett in 1993, 'is primarily against the father. ... In *Romeo and Juliet* there are two mother figures, the Nurse and Lady Capulet, but both have no power and both urge Juliet to compromise and obey her father' (p. 64). Capulet's patriarchal authority manifests itself in a variety of ways: as well as commanding his wife, he expects obedience from his daughter ('I think she will be ruled/In all respects by me; nay more, I doubt it not'; 3.4.14). He regards Juliet as a piece of property ('As you be mine, I'll give you to my friend'; 3.5.191) and accordingly commemorates her in 5.3 in terms of her dowry: 'This is my daughter's jointure, for no more/Can I demand' (5.3.296–7). But the most dramatic display of Capulet's power comes in his aggressive treatment of her in 3.5: he threatens her with physical violence ('speak not, reply not, do not answer me!/My fingers itch', 3.5.163–4), exploits her economic dependency by threatening to disown her, arguably a form of blackmail ('hang, beg, starve, die in the streets', 3.5.192), repeatedly insults her (proud, unworthy, mistress minion, green-sickness carrion, baggage, tallow-face, disobedient wretch, wretched puling fool, whining mammet, 3.5.143–84), and reduces her to the status of a domestic animal – 'fettle your fine joints' (l. 163); 'Graze where you will' (l. 188). Capulet resorts to insult, humiliation, even blackmail in order to procure his daughter's obedience; in Trevor Nunn's 1976 RSC production Capulet, played by John Woodvine, subjected his daughter to both mental and physical abuse in the scene (see fig. 2).

21

But *Romeo and Juliet* does not endorse Capulet's authoritarianism; rather, as Graham Holderness argues, 'everything in the text points to a critical response to his patriarchal bullying'.[18] Capulet is criticized for his behaviour: 'You are too hot' interrupts his wife (3.5.175). 'You are to blame, my lord, to rate her so' (l. 169), argues the Nurse, while Friar Lawrence suggests that 'The heavens do low'r upon you for some ill' (4.5.94), a criticism made more explicit in Q1 when the Friar reports that Capulet 'sought by *foule constraint*/To marrie her to Paris' (Q1, p. 97, emphasis added; see also Ch. 1). On the question of the arranged marriage, Shakespeare shows Capulet to be inconsistent, changing his mind within the space of two days: he initially tells Paris that 'My child is yet a stranger in the world' and 'My will to her consent is but a part' (1.2.8–19), but soon contradicts himself by seeking to enforce Juliet's marriage to Paris. This element of contradiction was added by Shakespeare to his source: in Brooke's *Romeus* the match with Paris isn't mentioned until after Romeo's banishment, and is initiated by a worried Lady Capulet who hopes it will 'banish care out of your daughters brest' (ll. 1844–53, p. 233); her gesture is well-intentioned, if misguided. As Coppelia Kahn has argued, 'by introducing the arranged marriage at the beginning, and by making Capulet change his mind about it, [Shakespeare] shows us how capricious patriarchal rule can be'.[19] Shakespeare also dramatizes the limitations of patriarchal rule by showing a daughter successfully defying and evading her father's authority. Juliet is outspoken in her resistance to Capulet ('tell my lord and father, madam,/I will not marry yet', 'Proud can I never be of what I hate', 3.5.120–1 and 147), capable of deceiving him ('Henceforward I am ever ruled by you', 4.2.21), and ultimately ignores his threats. The play dramatizes a daughter effectively undermining her father's power. In so doing the play engages with current debates about the due obedience of children and the limits of patriarchal power, relating it to *A Midsummer Night's Dream* (c. 1594–5), written in the same period as *Romeo and Juliet* and also revolving around a dispute between father and daughter over a projected marriage.

In practice, Capulet's characterization is open to interpretation. While John Woodvine emphasized his authoritarianism in Trevor Nunn's 1976 RSC production, in the 1978 BBC television

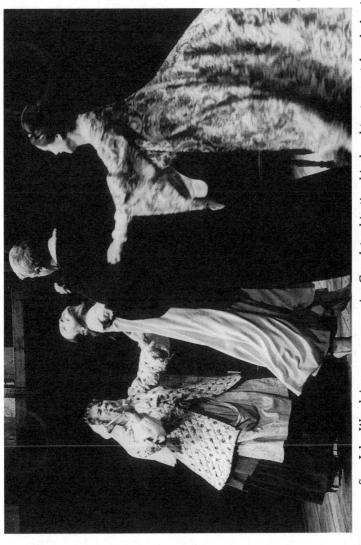

2 Act three, scene five: John Woodvine as an aggressive Capulet subjecting his daughter to mental and physical abuse in Trevor Nunn's 1976 RSC production. Notice how Lady Capulet looks on horrified and tries to intervene.

version Michael Horden's Capulet was 'socially incompetent but also likable'; 'his threats carry no menace ... the commands he gives even in his own house are neither received nor carried out by anyone'.[20] But Juliet's 'forefathers' remain a striking source of fear for her; indeed, her repeated allusions to the dead bodies of her male ancestors almost read like gothic horror (see the frontispiece);

> O, if I wake, shall I not be distraught,
> Environed with all these hideous fears,
> And madly play with my forefathers' joints,
> And pluck the mangled Tybalt from his shroud,
> And in this rage, with some great kinsman's bone,
> As with a club, dash out my desp'rate brains?

(4.3.49–54)

Juliet's 'hideous fears' around the dead, male body of the kinsman reveal the symbolic power of the father and kinsman, and arguably carry a curious note of incest (Nicholas Brooke goes so far as to claim that 'Juliet's feeling has arrived at full-scale necrophilia', p. 101). The passage can be compared with Mercutio's Queen Mab speech in that both speakers voice fantasies which border on the nightmarish: while Mercutio's anxiety is aroused by the body of the pregnant woman (see Ch. 3), Juliet's fear centres on the body of the dead forefather and kinsman.

While feminist criticism of *Romeo and Juliet* has tended to focus on the analysis of patriarchal power in the play, for late-nineteenth- and early-twentieth-century women critics the key point of interest was not patriarchy, but motherhood. 'The intercourse of mother and daughter', noted Constance O'Brien in 1879, 'is not one of Shakspere's favourite subjects; he only touches it twice [presumably a reference to *Romeo and Juliet* and *The Winter's Tale*], as if he was not quite sure of the ways of women together' (p. 143). Lady Capulet is claimed to represent a failure in motherhood, and her proposal of Juliet's marriage to Paris (1.3) – 'Tell me, daughter Juliet,/How stands your dispositions to be married?' (1.3.65–6) – is repeatedly cited as a critical moment in her maternal failings: 'she springs so important an event as marriage abruptly upon her only daughter', argued Jess Dorynne in 1913, 'as though she were suggesting a change in a dinner menu'.[21] Lady Capulet's lack of sympathy for her daughter was largely attributed to her 'cold, formal, propriety',[22] arguably embodied in the terms mother and daughter use to address each other which tend to denote status or deference rather than affection: 'daughter Juliet' (1.3.65), 'daughter' (3.5.64), 'girl' (3.5.79), 'ladyship' (3.5.106), 'Madam' (1.3.7; 3.5.68, 79, 85, 96, 111; 4.3.6; Juliet directly addresses Lady Capulet as her 'mother' only at 3.5.198).

Lady Capulet has more power as a mother than she does as a wife. In her first scene with Juliet (1.3), Lady Capulet issues orders to her daughter ('think of marriage now', 'Read o'er the volume of young Paris' face...Examine every married lineament'; 1.3.70 and 82–4), and Juliet responds with a display of filial obedience: 'no more deep will I endart mine eye/Than your consent gives strength to make it fly' (3.5.99–100). But Lady Capulet's maternal authority is soon disrupted: in 3.5 Juliet adopts a new, contestatory tone towards her ('I pray you tell my lord and father, madam,/I will not marry yet', 3.5.120–1), which Lady Capulet responds to by denying responsibility for her daughter: 'Do as thou wilt, for I have done with thee' (3.5.203). Juliet's pretence of obedience in their final scene together only serves to highlight Juliet's evasion of her mother's rule. *Romeo and Juliet* portrays a breakdown in matriarchal authority, and in the movement from filial obedience to disobedience charts a shift in power relations between mother and daughter.

This would have been of topical relevance to an Elizabethan audience: power struggles between mothers and daughters (particularly over an unmarried daughter's relations with men) were ongoing in early modern England. There are several examples from the period of aristocratic mothers wielding authority over their daughters – and of daughters circumventing their mother's power. Lady Anne Halkett, for instance, wrote that 'in the year 1644 I confess I was guilty of disobedience, for I gave way to the address of a person [Thomas Howard] whom my mother...had absolutely discharged me ever to allow of'.[23] Against her mother's orders Anne privately met Thomas, who confessed his undying love to her and 'provided a wedding ring and a minister to marry us' (p. 143). Anne's mother was 'incensed' at the proposal and forbade Anne from seeing Thomas again, but Anne secretly met him at night and continued the courtship. Her mother then threatened to disown her, saying 'she rather I were buried than bring so much ruin to the family she honored' (p. 150) – recalling Lady Capulet's line 'I would the fool were married to her grave' (3.5.140). Relations between mother and daughter grew worse until a kinsman, Sir Patrick Drummond, chastised Anne's mother for her 'severity' on 'unjust grounds', and mother and daughter were reconciled (p. 150–1).

Although Anne Halkett's diary was written some fifty years after Shakespeare's play, her illicit courtship and troubled relationship with her mother bear familiar traces to Juliet's, suggesting a continuity between *Romeo and Juliet* and historical practice. Both Shakespeare's play and Anne Halkett's diary record power struggles that took place between mother and daughter: the imposition and evasion of matriarchal authority; the deference to and disobedience of a mother; the denial of maternal affection, and the observation of a mother's 'severity'. This is not to say that mother–daughter relations in early modern England were generally poor: on the contrary, there are many counter examples of reciprocal and affectionate relations between mothers and daughters. Rather, *Romeo and Juliet* and Anne Halkett's diary record extreme cases of the breach between mother and daughter, and the breakdown of communication within the family.

In fact, Shakespeare's presentation of Lady Capulet is not necessarily as unsympathetic as has often been argued: she is an ambivalent figure open to conflicting interpretations. In 3.5 Lady Capulet arguably takes Juliet's side against her aggressive husband, interrupting and criticizing Capulet: 'Fie, fie, what, are you mad?', 'You are too hot' (ll. 157 and 175). In Trevor Nunn's 1976 RSC production, Lady Capulet looked on horrified at Capulet's violent treatment of Juliet and tried to intervene (see fig. 2). The 'lamentation scene' of 4.5, when the supposedly dead body of Juliet is discovered, offers another opportunity for the display of maternal affection, and in the 1978 BBC television version Lady Capulet's grief for her daughter is 'genuine'.[24] Notice how Lady Capulet's language in this scene is disjointed, marked by short phrases and repetition: 'O me, O me, my child, my only life!/Revive, look up, or I will die with thee./Help, help! Call help' (4.5.19–21). By contrast, Capulet launches immediately into an eloquent, elegaic mode: 'Death is my heir,/ My daughter he hath wedded. I will die,/ And leave him all' (4.5.38–40). For Susan Bassnett the grief of Juliet's mother 'is for the loss of a child, whilst her father's grief is couched in terms of loss of inheritance' (p. 64). While Helena Faucit and Jess Dorynne found the interaction between mother and daughter in 1.3 cold, hard, and brutal, Lady Capulet can be played as affectionate, even intimate, towards her daughter. In Simon Parry's 1996 New End Theatre production (London), Lady Capulet took Juliet in her arms as she broached the topic of marriage; Juliet shared in her mother and nurse's infectious enthusiasm at the prospect of Paris as a husband, and Lady Capulet's questions were gently asked and genuinely concerned: 'How stands your dispositions to be married?', 'can you love the gentleman?', 'can you like of Paris' love?' (1.3.66, 80 and 97). In fact this scene is developed differently in the alternative Elizabethan texts of *Romeo and Juliet*, the First Quarto (Q1, published in 1597) and the Second Quarto (Q2, published in 1599; see Ch. 1). As Steven Urkowitz has argued 'both Juliet and her mother perform significantly different actions in these alternative texts': while in Q1 Lady Capulet 'delicately introduces the topic of marriage to her daughter' and Juliet is 'excited' at her mother's proposal, Q2 'presents Lady Capulet as a hard-driving advocate for Paris' and suggests 'the child's reticence, an unwillingness to plunge into the high-pressure whirl of Veronese sexuality' (pp. 298–9).

There are in fact three mother figures in *Romeo and Juliet*: Lady Capulet, Lady Montague, and the Nurse – arguably the most maternal figure in the play. I examine the character and functions of the Nurse and contemporary practices of wet-nursing in more detail in Chapter 3; here I want to call attention to the Nurse's role as a surrogate mother. By contrast to Lady Capulet, the Nurse dwells upon her maternal body, recalling memories of breastfeeding Juliet (1.3.27–69). It is not only milk but affection that is withheld, displaced and transferred between these three women. Having lost her own daughter (Susan), the Nurse seems to transfer her affection to Juliet, and Juliet reciprocates; Brenda Bruce, playing the part of the Nurse with the RSC in 1980, argues that the Nurse 'is in fact the Mother, the person in whom Juliet lays her trust and confides her secret love'.[25] The intimacy between the Nurse and Juliet is indicated in their affectionate addresses to each other: lamb, ladybird (1.3.3), honey Nurse, good sweet Nurse (2.5.18 and 21), good, good Nurse (2.5.28), wench (2.5.43), sweet, sweet, sweet Nurse (2.5.53), Honest Nurse (2.5.77), gentle Nurse (4.2.1), lamb, slug-a-bed, love, sweet heart (4.5.2–3). Juliet displaces her filial affection from her natural mother to her Nurse. Indeed, the Nurse gains Juliet's confidence to become a rival mother to Lady Capulet – wielding more influence, and so power, over Juliet than Lady Capulet. Surrogate motherhood parallels the dynamics of fatherhood in *Romeo and Juliet*. While Montague is unaware of the 'cause' of Romeo's sorrow the Friar has been acting as Romeo's confidant, and in criticizing Romeo 'for doting' (2.3.83) the Friar has already delivered the 'good counsel' which Montague sought to provide himself for his son (1.1.133). It is the Friar, not Montague, whom Romeo consults about his intended marriage. The Friar becomes a surrogate father for Romeo, and in so doing effectively rivals the patriarchal authority of Montague. Indeed, *Romeo and Juliet* arguably revolves around a series of substitutions: a Juliet for a Rosaline (see the Chorus, 1.5.144–57, and Ch. 4); a Nurse for a Mother; a Friar for a father; a Paris for a Romeo; a deathbed for a bridal bed (see Ch. 4).

Capulet and Lady Capulet enact multiple roles in their household as both husband and father, wife and mother (indeed Lady Capulet is variously described in speech prefixes in Q1 and Q2 as wife, mother, Capulet's Wife, Lady, Lady of the house, and, confusingly, Old Lady). The couple share seven scenes together, yet because criticism of *Romeo and Juliet* tends to focus overwhelmingly on the two protagonists the Capulets' marriage has often been overlooked. Capulet and Lady Capulet are often assumed to be of the same age but the text(s) of *Romeo and Juliet* do not point to this notional middle-aged married couple: while 'Old Capulet' (as he is frequently described in stage directions) reminisces about masking as a young man some 'thirty years' ago (1.5.30–2), the play points out quite carefully that Lady Capulet was a teenage mother – 'By my count,' she tells Juliet, 'I was your mother much upon these years/That you are now a maid' (1.3.72–4). This makes for a generation gap between husband and wife (indeed, Capulet is conceivably old enough to be Lady Capulet's father), inviting attention towards the disparities operating in their marriage.

On the one hand, Capulet dominates his wife, overruling her in setting the date for Juliet's marriage (4.2.38–9), issuing orders ('Wife, go you to her ere you go to bed . . . mark you me?' 3.4.14–17), and ignoring her interjections to control his anger (3.5.157, 175). In their longest scene together (3.5) Lady Capulet arguably capitulates to Capulet: her response to Juliet's refusal to marry Paris is to confer the issue to her husband ('Here comes your father, tell him so yourself; / And see how he will take it at your hands'; 3.5.124–5). Lady Capulet perhaps has little choice but to allow her husband the dominant hand in the household – and in this sense we might view her as a younger woman dominated, silenced, and suppressed by her older husband (indeed, in 1913 Jess Dorynne claimed she was the most tragic figure in the play, p. 93). This is how Simon Parry's 1996 production of *Romeo and Juliet* (New End Theatre, London) portrayed their marriage: Lady Capulet was cast as some twenty years the junior of her husband, resigned to taking orders from him, clearly afraid of his temper and anxious to avoid his wrath. In his company, she became vulnerable – a victim, like Juliet, of Capulet's temper and authoritarianism. In so doing the production raised problems of domestic violence within marriage, and problematized the notion of the Capulets' marriage as a partnership, and their treatment of Juliet as jointly enacted. A similar sense of the scene was achieved in Trevor Nunn's 1976 RSC production (see fig. 2); Zeffirelli's film (1968) hinted at the Capulets' unhappy marriage, while Michael Bogdanov's 1986 RSC production insinuated an affair between Lady Capulet and Tybalt – a suggestion also developed in Luhrmann's 1996 film. Indeed, Luhrmann gave Lady Capulet a first name, Gloria, and an unhappy character history:

> she's fairly high-strung, is in a repressed relationship, is probably lonely, feels that her husband doesn't love her and her daughter is growing up and their relationship is strained, but she can't really change her situation because her role is that of a decorative, obedient bride.[26]

But this view of Capulet's domination of Lady Capulet – of the subjugation of the wife – can also be challenged. Feminist literary criticism has sought to examine not only the submission of women under patriarchal rule but the ways in which women resisted or negotiated the restrictions placed upon them – acting as agents not victims in their personal relations. We might then reread the Capulets' marriage as one in which a struggle for power takes place, with Lady Capulet adopting a contestatory position towards her husband. Indeed, this is hinted at in their first appearance on stage (an episode absent from Q1):

> CAPULET What noise is this? Give me my long sword, ho!
> LADY CAPULET A crutch, a crutch! why call you for a sword?
> CAPULET My sword, I say!

(1.1.66–9)

With her sarcastic (or, more generously, witty) intervention, Lady Capulet challenges Capulet's action and behaviour; moreover, as 'sword' meant penis in contemporary sexual slang, she arguably slurs his virility by suggesting his 'sword' is redundant. Her interjections in 3.5 can be interpreted not as ineffective pleas but bold criticism of a husband's behaviour; 'Fie, fie, what, are you mad?' (3.5.157; absent from Q1), 'Fie, fie you are too hot' (3.5.175). Later in the play Lady Capulet threatens to put Capulet under her surveillance – 'Ay, you have been a mouse-hunt in your time,/But I will watch you from such watching now' (4.4.11–12; a threat omitted from Q1) – reversing what has been described as the 'patriarchal gaze', in which women are subject to men's surveillance and frame their behaviour to meet male expectations. This sense of Lady Capulet's contestatory relationship with her husband becomes especially noticeable when we compare the text of Q1 (traditionally discredited as unauthoritative) with Q2 (on which most modern editions of the play are based). While Q1 minimizes Lady Capulet's interjections and differences with her husband, Q2 expands her contestatory, critical role (especially in the lines 1.1.67, 3.5.157 and 4.4.12), and in so doing injects more complexity into the dynamics of power between husband and wife.

Complexity is also the keynote of early modern marital relations. On the one hand orthodox ideology stressed the authoritative rule of the husband over the wife: for instance, the *Homily of the State of Matrimony* (1563), intended 'to be read in every parish Church agreeably', commanded wives to 'obey your own husband', 'cease from commanding and perform subjection', and told husbands 'the woman is a frail vessel and thou art therefore made the ruler and head over her'.[27] In 1977 the historian Lawrence Stone argued that the elite 'internalized' expectations of 'authority and respect by the husband and father, and of submission, obedience and deference by the wife and the children' (p. 146). But Stone's account of family relations in early modern England has recently been criticized. As Keith Wrightson explains, although 'woman's subordination was axiomatic':

> Conventional definition of roles and the actual performance of them in everyday life can be quite different things. ... The picture which emerges indicates the *private* existence of a strong complementary and companionate ethos, side by side with, and often overshadowing, theoretical adherence to the doctrine of male authority and *public* female subordination.[28]

Moreover, husbands had duties towards as well as authority over their wives, and partnership, mutuality, and tolerance in marriage were recognized to be crucial to its success: as William Perkins argued in 1609, the first duty of the husband was 'to honor his wife' and 'love her as himself', treating her 'as his companion or yoke-fellow...because God did not make her subject to him as a servant'.[29] For an Elizabethan audience attuned to contemporary debates about ideals and practices of patriarchal authority within marriage, the Capulets might make a far more interesting dramatic couple than modern critics have tended to allow.

Romeo and Juliet was written at a time when family relations were being negotiated, contested, and defined. Since the 1980s Renaissance literary critics have been increasingly concerned with the relationship between literature and history, and two recent critical movements, new historicism and cultural materialism, have been particularly influential in examining the early modern cultural contexts of Shakespeare's plays. Both are interested in the operations of power and both assume that literary texts, far from 'transcending' their age, are grounded in their historical context(s) – and thus are not properly speaking 'universal'. In general terms, while new historicist critics have tended to stress the imposition of power and authority (particularly that of the state), cultural materialist critics emphasize the negotiation or subversion of power.[30] Applied to *Romeo and Juliet*, a new historicist reading might emphasize the imposition and dominance of patriarchal rule, whereby both mother and daughter have to observe obedience to Capulet, while a cultural materialist reading might focus instead upon resistance to that rule. In my view *Romeo and Juliet* not only examines but is critical of the abuse of a husband's and father's power: the play portrays a crisis in patriarchal authority.

That crisis also extends to the feud, and here I want briefly to note two aspects of the operation of patriarchy in the feud: first, the politics of naming in the play, and secondly the assertion of civic, patriarchal authority. Juliet recognizes the symbolic power of the father's name when she asks Romeo to 'deny thy father and refuse thy name... 'Tis but thy name that is my enemy/ Thou art thyself, though not a Montague' (2.2.34–9). As Coppelia Kahn has argued:

> in the feud, names (the signs of patriarchal authority and allegiance) are calls to arms....for Romeo to refuse his name – to separate himself from the feud – he would have to deny his father... his new identity as a man is to be based on his allegiance to her as her husband and not on his allegiance to his father. (pp. 343–4)

But ultimately the feudal father figures, Capulet and Montague, have to submit to the authority of Prince Escales, and the aggressive protection of family identity and honour gives way to the preservation of civic identity and honour. Indeed, for Dympna Callaghan, the struggle between household fathers (Capulet and Montague), church fathers (Friar Lawrence), and civic fathers (Escales) animates the whole play:

> the *shifting configurations* of patriarchal law and the changing formations of desire which attend it comprise the structure and substance of Shakespeare's text. In this sense, the play articulates a crisis in patriarchy itself – specifically the transference of power from the feuding fathers to the Prince. (p. 72)

While Escales struggles to assert himself as 'the preeminent patriarchal power in Verona' (p. 74), Capulet and Montague emerge as infantile and childish; as Susan Bassnett points out, 'the breakdown of the relationship between parents and children in the domestic arena is paralleled by the breakdown of the relationship between ruler and subjects' (p. 69). When we first see Escales he has to struggle to make himself heard ('Will they not hear?', 1.1.74) and his orders for discipline (issued in 1.1 and 3.1) are ignored. But in the final scene Escales reasserts his authority; indeed, David Levaux's 1991 RSC production ended with 'the stark re-emergence of the power of Escalus' as 'an absolute ruler'[31] (see Ch. 4). Certainly as Callaghan points out, Escales assumes control over the narrative of the love tragedy: he takes Romeo's letter intended for his father ('Give me the letter. I will look on it'; 5.3.275-8) and in so doing 'symbolically absorbs the power of Romeo's father'. He authorizes Romeo's account of events, and:

> in taking the role of coordinator and interpreter of the various renditions of the tragic events in the play's coda (the Friar's, Balthasar's), the Prince consolidates his power over the errant feudal forces that have previously sought to dissipate it. (pp. 78-9)

Peter Smith, commenting on Levaux's 1991 RSC production, pushes this idea of 'consolidation' a stage further: 'someone has to write history and, as *Nineteen Eighty-Four* makes plain, they that control the past control the future' (p. 128). But how far Escales' power finally resembles that of 'Big Brother' is, of course, a matter of contention. Plays are more than their endings, and in my view *Romeo and Juliet* focuses more on rivalry between civic, household and church fathers than upon the absolute power of the state – and in so doing the play exposes fragility, instability and conflict in structures of patriarchal authority (structures, at least, imagined in sixteenth-century England and projected onto fifteenth-century Italy). In exploring relations between politics, patriarchy, and passion, *Romeo and Juliet* reveals, perhaps above all, the interconnection of public and private domains.

3

Constructing Identities

The construction of personal identity is a social process. History, society, and culture shape though not entirely determine the ways in which men and women perceive themselves and are perceived by others. In *Romeo and Juliet* personal identity is inflected by distinctions of gender, class, age, and ethnicity. The play also shows how personal identity may be conflicted; put under pressure from opposing demands and desires. When Romeo, for instance, fails to respond to Tybalt's taunts in 3.1, Romeo's new and as yet private identity as a husband and Capulet-by-marriage conflicts with that of the aggressive, partisan man expected of him: the scene stages a struggle between the needs of private and public manhood; between privately fashioned and socially sanctioned identities. Such conflicts of identity are grounded in early modern society: *Romeo and Juliet* plays upon and engages with contemporary cultural practices and concerns.

An analysis of 'character' in *Romeo and Juliet* should not, then, be restricted to a discussion of personality traits. One of the problems with traditional Shakespearian 'character criticism' is that it tends to suppress an analysis of *characterization* (how a character is constructed, and to what effect), and ignores the fact that in performance a character may be infinitely varied. In fact the dramatic conventions that Shakespeare inherited in the late-sixteenth century were concerned less with psychological realism than with the *function* of characters and character 'types' as vehicles for exploring ideas; as a means to an end. As Margot Heinemann argues, paraphrasing Brecht, 'Shakespeare's theatre was more concerned with telling stories, whereas modern interpreters ... concentrate on making us share the inner life of the character' (p. 234). If we restrict a discussion of character to personality traits, then the underlying stories of a dramatic text may be left untold. Furthermore, characters in *Romeo and Juliet* are multidimensional, embodying and evoking a variety of ideas, images, and issues, and are open to alternative readings. The 'stories' I want to attend to in this chapter deal with how personal identity in *Romeo and Juliet* is shaped by distinctions of gender, sexuality, age, social status, and ethnicity operating both in the play and in early modern culture at large.

PUBLIC AND PRIVATE SPACE

Romeo and Juliet is marked by careful attention to contrasts and conflict between public and private. Not only do characters behave differently in public and private (perhaps, above all, Juliet), but the play moves between public and private spaces – streets, gardens, houses, reception rooms, bedchambers, monastic cells, churchyards, tombs. Different characters have different access to these spaces according to their gender and status; indeed, *Romeo and Juliet* enacts a politics of space that is rooted in early modern cultural practice.

Romeo and Juliet is a domestic tragedy, and the private setting of the household arguably comes to dominate the play (especially acts two and four). Within the household, Shakespeare distinguishes between public and private rooms, ranging from the 'great chamber' (1.5.12) in which the masque takes place and the servants' quarters (the pastry or pantry, and kitchen), to the most intimate and strictly controlled room within the household, Juliet's bedchamber (Juliet also invites the Nurse to join her in her closet: a very small, private room increasingly built into the recesses of Elizabethan houses, 4.2.32). Capulet's household is depicted in more precise detail than the street, particularly in the Second Quarto (or Q2) of the play. The preparations for the masque, for instance (Q2 only, 1.5.1–13), involve four household servants and an array of contemporary household goods: napkins, trenchers (wooden plates), join-stools (wooden stools fitted by a joiner), court-cupboards (sideboards), plate (silverware), marchpane (marzipan). Attention is drawn to the material provision of Juliet's marriage feast (see especially 4.2.9 and 37), and there are repeated references to household goods: ornaments from Juliet's closet (4.2.32–3), herbs, keys, spices, dates, quinces (Q2 only, 4.4.1–2), baked meats, things for the cook, drier logs, spits, baskets (4.4.5–17), beds and curtains (Q1, pp. 85 and 87). At the same time, attention is drawn to the labour of the household: giving household orders; moving, washing, and scraping trenchers; clearing furniture; serving supper in the great chamber; tidying tables; tending the fire; fetching foodstuffs; cooking; making beds; getting dressed. The effect of these layers of household detail is to emphasize the domestic context of the play; by contrast, Shakespeare's principal source for the play, Brooke's *Romeus*, pays little attention to servants and household goods or management. The household becomes the symbolic centre of Shakespeare's play – a bold choice for a tragedy, which traditionally was the stuff of kings, politicians, and generals; courts, governments, and battlefields (see Ch. 2).

As an elite, unmarried girl, Juliet is restricted in her movements: as the Chorus puts it, compared to Romeo, Juliet has the opportunity or 'means much less/To meet her new-beloved anywhere' (1.5.154–5). She does not venture beyond the household except to go to confession – for which she needs permission ('Have you got leave to go to shrift today?', 2.5.65). As such she conforms to the orthodox model of feminine behaviour put forward by contemporary moralists that women should stay within the confines of the home. According to conduct literature (writing on how to behave) only privacy and enclosure ensured the chastity of wives and daughters: thus in *The English Gentlewoman* (London, 1631) Richard Brathwaite urged women to remain 'in your Chambers or private Closets...retired from the eyes of men' (p. 47). Georgianna Ziegler has described this confinement of women as 'a kind of domestic enclosure created by a patriarchal feudal society, afraid both of the weakness and of the insidious power of women' (p. 74). In other words, fears circulating in patriarchal society about uncontrolled female sexuality led to women being confined to the home. There are many historical examples of women being curtailed by their fathers and husbands. But there were also occasions when enclosure – or more precisely the privacy it afforded – could become enabling for women. Thus it is precisely in the space of her bedchamber that Juliet undermines Capulet's patriarchal authority by consummating her illicit marriage to Romeo (and later by taking the Friar's potion). Juliet's room is the site of independence and disobedience, as well as restriction and enclosure. Privacy enables Juliet's expression of subjectivity – that is, her sense of her self. In fact she enacts Brathwaite's concern that 'privacy is made the recluse of *Temptation*.... Therefore doe nothing *privately*, which you would not doe *publickly*' (pp. 44–9).

Romeo and Juliet distinguishes between the freedom of movement for unmarried girls and for married women: Juliet's mother, like Lady Montague, moves beyond the household to join her husband when 'brawls' erupt on the streets (1.1.65 and 3.1.131), while the widowed, lower-status Nurse apparently enjoys the most freedom of movement among women in the play, facilitating her role as a mediator between Romeo and Juliet. The younger and older male generations inhabit both the private domain of the home and the public domain of the street; indeed, the street becomes identified with men and the feud (see 1.1.8–17 and 3.1.43–7). Mercutio confirms the necessary publicity – among men – of feuding aggression when he rejects Benvolio's plea to 'withdraw unto some private place': 'Men's eyes were made to look, and let them gaze' (3.1.43–7). Similarly, Capulet is keen to fight on the street ('Give me my long sword, ho!', 1.1.66) but not prepared to resume the feud in his own home: 'I would not for the wealth of all this town/Here in my house do him disparagement' (1.5.68–9). If Juliet's bedchamber becomes the site of private rebellion, then the streets of Verona are the site of public rebellion between feuding families.

Romeo moves between these two sites; indeed, he is the character with most freedom of movement in the play (whether licit or illicit, chosen or imposed). Unlike his male peers, Romeo is strongly associated with private space in the play: at the outset of the play he voluntarily 'pens' (encloses) himself in his chamber (1.1.129) and, performing the part of the male love-melancholic, he withdraws into the 'covert' of woods, glades, and gardens (1.1.116; see Ch. 2). After meeting Juliet, Romeo's cultivation of solitude gives way to the pursuit of his private desires ('satisfaction' with Juliet) – and, as a result, private space – particularly Juliet's bedchamber – becomes increasingly associated in the play with intrigue rather than solitude. While men were typically identified as 'public' beings in early modern culture, *Romeo and Juliet* complicates those stereotypes by showing a man who (by contrast to his male peers) cultivates privacy as part of his persona and inhabits private spaces.

In this politics of space, thresholds become significant. *Romeo and Juliet* pays special attention to questions of access (perhaps most memorably in the so-called 'balcony scene'), and to the objects that variously impede or aid entry: walls, windows, rope ladders, mattocks, wrenching irons, spades. In order to gain access to Juliet, Romeo has first to cross the threshold of the 'orchard wall' (2.1.5), 'high and hard to climb' (2.2.63), and penetrate the Capulet estate. The orchard becomes what social anthropologists have described as a liminal space – a space or period of time in which normal social conventions are temporarily deferred, ignored, or challenged. Not only does Romeo break the convention of the feud, collapsing the boundaries between Montague and Capulet by meeting Juliet, but Juliet breaks the conventions of courtship by assuming the dominant role normally ascribed to men ('I should have been more strange, I must confess', 2.2.102). The space of the orchard is also invested with sexual symbolism. 'Of all the symbols Shakespeare uses to denote sexual activity and sexual rites of passage in the plays', notes Marjorie Garber, 'the most traditional of all is the walled garden':

> The traditional biblical description of the bride as a *hortus conclusus*, a 'garden inclosed' (Song of Songs, 4:12), becomes in his plays a geographical emblem of virginity and a locus for sexual initiation. The terms 'garden' and 'orchard' at this period both refer to an enclosed plot of land devoted to horticulture; 'orchard' derives etymologically from Latin *hortus* and Anglo-Saxon *yard*. It is in such settings in the plays, almost inevitably, that love is sworn and affections given.[1]

Although 2.2 has become popularly known as the 'balcony scene' following eighteenth-century stage conventions, the texts of *Romeo and Juliet* do not specify a balcony but a window. The threshold between Romeo and Juliet is a window ('what light through yonder window breaks?', 2.2.2); a physical barrier, the window evokes, indeed becomes symbolic of, the social barriers against Romeo and Juliet's relationship. Thus one of the most strategic props in the play becomes the rope ladder – 'the cords'

(3.2.33 and 35) which allow Romeo access to Juliet's bedchamber. Juliet's window comes to mark a threshold in her relations with Romeo: once he gains entry to her window with the rope ladder, he also gains entry to her body.

BODY POLITICS

Romeo and Juliet is a play obsessed with bodies and body parts. The play's bawdy humour draws attention to the male and female body (especially genitalia); characters repeatedly discuss their physical well-being or ailments, and dwell upon bodily functions: sleeping, eating, drinking, making love, pregnancy, breastfeeding. The body is figured in complex ways in *Romeo and Juliet* – as old, young, impotent, virile, sexual, maternal, healthy, diseased. Indeed, it is fear of the diseased body that underpins the tragic turn of events in the final act of the play. Friar John reports that Friar Lawrence's letter to Romeo was not delivered in Mantua because of the plague: 'So fearful were they of infection' (5.2.16). This is one of several references to plague in the play (see also 1.4.74–6, 1.5.15–16, 3.1.82 and 91, 3.2.90) which would have had topical relevance for an Elizabethan audience: in 1593, not long before the first performance of *Romeo and Juliet*, plague in London was so bad that the theatres were closed down and Elizabeth I's court removed to St Albans (Hertfordshire).

The diseased or impotent body also inflects Shakespeare's portrayal of sexuality in the play. In the opening scene of the play Lady Capulet sarcastically draws attention to her husband's impotence – both martially and sexually – by remarking that his 'sword' (slang for penis) should be substituted for a 'crutch' (1.1.67). There are several implicit allusions to symptoms of venereal disease in the play, including bone-ache – suffered by the Nurse ('Fie, how my bones ache! What a jaunce have I!', 2.5.26) and alluded to by Mercutio ('O their bones, their bones!', 2.4.30–1) – and blistered lips ('the angry Mab with blisters plagues', 1.4.75). Sexuality in the play thus emerges not only as virile, fertile, youthful, virginal, passionate, and indeed exploitative, but as potentially disease-ridden and debilitating. Other images of disease in the play are clustered around lovesickness (see especially 1.1.185–93), old age, infection and poison, even food disorders. Capulet attacks Juliet in 3.5 by calling her 'green-sickness carrion!' (3.5.156–7), an allusion to a perceived illness associated with food disorders which adolescent girls – otherwise known as 'green' girls (see *Hamlet*, 1.3.101) – were thought to suffer from (as such it has been compared with modern-day anorexia nervosa and bulimia). The accumulative effect of these references to the sick, diseased body in Shakespeare's *Romeo and Juliet* is to suggest the precarious social, as well as physical, health of Verona.

It is, however, the portrayal of the grotesque and the maternal body in the play that I want to focus upon here. In his analysis of the 'habits' of the Renaissance body, Mikhail Bakhtin argued for an opposition in early modern culture between the 'classical' and the 'grotesque' body. The classical body denoted a clean, controlled, and ordered body; an image of 'finished, completed' man.[2] In *Romeo and Juliet*, the chaste figure of Rosaline, closed to outside advances, perhaps best corresponds to the classical body (see. 1.1.202–5). The grotesque body, by contrast, is 'unfinished, outgrows itself, transgresses its own limits', and is concerned

> with the lower stratum of the body, the life of the body, and the reproductive organs: it therefore relates to acts of defecation and copulation, conception, pregnancy and birth. (pp. 21 and 26)

Thus the grotesque emphasizes those parts of the body 'that are open to the outside world', 'the open mouth, the genital organs, the breasts, the phallus, the potbelly, the nose' (p. 26)

Much of the bawdy humour in *Romeo and Juliet* revolves around the grotesque body (Ch. 4). As Knowles points out (pp. 71–4), the Nurse seems to epitomize Bakhtin's notion of the grotesque, especially in her repeated allusions to copulation, conception, genitalia, and her own body. Her opening line reveals that she lost her virginity 'at twelve year old' (1.3.2); she proceeds to joke about Juliet falling backwards, inviting sex (1.3.43 and 57–8), and casually refers to 'a young cock'rel's stone', or testicle (1.3.54). During the course of the play the Nurse seems to take a vicarious pleasure in anticipating Juliet's sexual encounters. After announcing Romeo's proposed marriage to Juliet she immediately imagines Juliet's sexual activity: the 'wanton blood' rising in her cheeks; the 'bird's nest' (suggestive of pubic hair) which Romeo 'must climb', Juliet's bearing of 'the burden' of Romeo's body while making love (2.5.70–5). The Nurse effectively collapses marriage with sex, a move she repeats in act four when speaking of Juliet's marriage with Paris in terms of sexual exertion:

> I warrant
> The County Paris has set up his rest
> That you shall rest but little.
>
> . . . .
>
> Ay let the County take you in your bed,
> He'll fright you up, i'faith.

(4.5.5–11)

By contrast, Lady Capulet presents Juliet's marriage to Paris as a romantic experience – 'the golden story' (1.3.93) – while Capulet considers the marriage principally in terms of social and economic status: 'of noble parentage,/Of fair demesnes, youthful and nobly ligned' (3.5.179–80). Bakhtin argued that the grotesque mode could be used to counteract or undermine the status of the 'classical', high, or orthodox; it can puncture the gravity and grasp of dominant discourses and ideologies (systems of belief and expression). Applied to the Nurse, we might say that her discourse of sex challenges, and arguably undermines, the idealization of romantic love voiced by Lady Capulet (and indeed Juliet) and the notion that marriage is principally a status issue, voiced by Capulet. While the Capulets mask the presence of sexuality within marriage, the Nurse exposes it.

Romeo and Juliet is also striking for its insistence upon the maternal body – which recalls the grotesque's emphasis upon 'copulation, conception, pregnancy and birth'.[3] Conception is hinted at in the opening Prologue ('the fatal loins' of the Capulets and Montagues, 5), and reiterated in the repeated punning in the play on the word *bear* (to bear the weight of a man while making love, and to bear children). The Nurse anticipates Juliet's pregnancy ('bigger women grow by men'; 1.3.96); Lady Capulet calls attention to the reproductive potential of her daughter's body (1.3.73–4), while Juliet describes her love for Romeo as a 'Prodigious birth' (1.5.139). The Nurse talks about breastfeeding with humour, frankness, and intimacy, casually describing the contemporary practice of

41

putting wormwood (a bitter plant) on her nipple in order to wean Juliet: 'When it did taste the wormwood on the nipple / Of my dug, and felt it bitter, pretty fool, / To see it tetchy and fall out wi'th'dug!' (1.3.30–3). Her vivid description of the episode, coupled with the presence it holds in her mind – 'I never shall forget it' (1.3.25) – indicate her self-identification as a nursing mother (hardly surprising given her profession). By contrast, Lady Capulet barely refers to her maternal body, remarking only to Juliet that 'I was your mother much upon these years / That you are now a maid' (1.3.73–4). 'There is no atmosphere of maternal tenderness about this lady', concluded Jess Dorynne in 1913 (p. 73) – but perhaps Lady Capulet is simply conforming to the cultural imperative of the closed, ordered, 'classical' body, and enacting the due feminine modesty demanded of elite women. By contrast, the lower-status Nurse is able to make free reference to her nipples and breasts with less threat of impropriety, and in this respect the maternal body in *Romeo and Juliet* seems figured along class lines.

While the Nurse speaks literally of breastfeeding, the Friar speaks metaphorically of Nature as a nursing mother:

> The earth that's nature's mother is her tomb;
> What is her burying grave, that is her womb;
> And from her womb children of divers kind
> We sucking on her natural bosom find.

> (2.3.9–12)

For Edward Snow, Friar Lawrence imagines nature arrested at the maternal breast (p. 187). But the Friar also articulates one of the play's central motifs – the womb/tomb – and foreshadows the final scene in which an actual 'tomb' becomes the 'burying grave' of the 'children' of Capulet and Montague.[4] When Romeo comes to deploy the womb/tomb motif in act five, his imagery is not of nourishment but of devouring and engulfment:

> Thou detestable maw, thou womb of death,
> Gorged with the dearest morsel of the earth,
> Thus I enforce thy rotten jaws to open,
> And in despite I'll cram thee with more food.

> (5.3.45–9)

Romeo associates the womb/tomb with a 'detestable maw' – the mouth or throat of a voracious, wild animal. There are intriguing sexual undertones here, for it was commonplace to characterize women's sexual desire in terms of a voracious, animalistic appetite, while contemporary medical treatises characterized the womb as a hungry, moving organ that wandered around the woman's body on a monthly cycle. Romeo's imagery effectively associates the womb with a fierce animal's hunger and death (the tomb). But his forced entry of the Capulet tomb also evokes images of rape or sexual intercourse. Romeo 'enforces' the womb/tomb open and stuffs it ('cram', penetrate) with his own body. A few minutes later Friar Lawrence looks on the tomb and exclaims 'Alack, alack, what blood is this which stains/The stony entrance of this sepulchre?' (5.3.140–1), and, as Coppelia Kahn has suggestively argued, 'the blood-spattered entrance to this tomb that has been figured as a womb recalls both a defloration or initiation into sexuality and a birth' (p. 353).

While the opening acts of the play tend to stress the generation and nourishment of the maternal body, the womb increasingly becomes fashioned as a source of fear, threat, and insecurity. A sense of foreboding is arguably the keynote to Mercutio's speech upon the 'midwife' Queen Mab (an image which both alludes to Queen Mab's role assisting in the birth of fantasies and underscores the repeated reference to the maternal body in the play):

> This is the hag, when maids lie on their backs,
> That presses them and learns them first to bear,
> Making them women of good carriage. This is she –
>
> (1.4.91–3)

Mercutio describes a mechanistic account of heterosexual sex in which women are merely sexual and reproductive objects, a vehicle ('carriage') for bearing men and children. Coppelia Kahn has read these lines as revealing Mercutio's 'fear of giving in to the seething nighttime world of unconscious desires associated with the feminine' (p. 343); that is, the sexual desires that women may arouse in men. This note of latent eroticism in the speech is certainly hinted at in Henry Fuseli's extraordinary painting of *Fairy Mab* engraved by W. Raddon (fig. 3): a plump, long-haired young woman in a low-cut dress holds a cup against her breast and looks out seductively, mouth open, from a dark

3 *Fairy Mab* (1.4.53), engraved by W. Raddon after a painting by Henry Fuseli. Notice the black maidservant with a knowing smile and the hookah (used for inhaling tobacco and drugs) on the table: Fuseli's Mab fuses the erotic with the exotic.

corner; on a table beside her is a hookah (used for inhaling tobacco and drugs) while to her other side a black woman-servant stands by with a knowing smile on her face. Fuseli's *Fairy Mab* fuses the erotic with the exotic. But Mercutio's Queen Mab speech also carries a note of phobia – a fear of and fascination with the maternal body. His use of the word 'hag' – an incubus or nightmare that induced evil, particularly sexual, dreams – sounds a note of revulsion: women's conception and pregnancy become part of a nightmarish vision for Mercutio. This was the tone of both Zeffirelli's 1968 film and Luhrmann's 1996 film: Mercutio became progressively disturbed during the Queen Mab speech and Romeo's interruption, 'Peace, peace, Mercutio, peace!' (1.4.95) was said in the manner of a parent calming down a child after a bad dream (or, in the case of Luhrmann's film, a bad trip on hallucinogenic drugs). Terry Hands's 1973 RSC production deliberately emphasized the latent misogyny and sexual anxiety of the Queen Mab speech (see fig. 4): Mercutio carried 'a grotesque, coarse-featured, life-size female doll, upon which he vented clearly sado-masochistic sexual loathing' that was both 'deeply-disturbed and equally disturbing'.[5]

What should we make of the play's insistent allusions to the maternal body? On the one hand, in his opening speech on Mother Nature, Friar Lawrence posits an alternative teleology (or way of thinking) to the patriarchal, male-centred codes which seem to dominate the play. Whereas the feud fosters enmity and death and is centred upon the figure of the father ('Deny thy father and refuse thy name', 2.2.34), the Friar appeals to maternal nourishment and invests the maternal body with positive, generative attributes. On the other hand it could be argued that women in the play are repeatedly reduced to their reproductive functions, and regarded as objects rather than subjects. In this respect, the maternal body becomes used to position and effectively disempower women. Alternatively, Coppelia Kahn has suggestively argued that adolescent motherhood becomes an adolescent rite of passage 'typical for youth in Verona' – a rite which, by committing suicide, Juliet rejects (p. 349). The maternal body thus becomes a cultural imperative for young women that is encouraged by both older men and women (witness Lady Capulet's insistence that Juliet is

45

4   Mercutio (Bernard Lloyd) in the Queen Mab speech (1.4.53–94),
playing up the bawdy and unleashing sadomasochistic sexual loathing
(and desire?) on a coarse-featured life-size female doll in
Terry Hands's 1973 production for the RSC.

old enough to be a mother). Or we might emphasize instead the element of the 'grotesque': the play's insistent allusions to conception, pregnancy, and birth, as well as to big bellies (1.3.96) and breasts, share in grotesque humour and its 'material bodily principle',[6] undermining the idealization and romanticization of desire in the play.

Alternatively, psychoanalytic critic Janet Adelman has argued that the maternal body was a source of male anxiety and psychological trauma in early modern England. 'Culturally constructed as literally dangerous to everyone, the maternal body must have seemed especially dangerous to little boys', who had to form their 'specifically masculine selfhood against the matrix of [their mother's] overwhelming femaleness' (p. 7). Wet-nursing (which Adelman provocatively describes as 'sometimes tantamount to murder') effectively prolonged the period of 'infantile dependency' when male infants 'were subject to pleasures and dangers especially associated with nursing and the maternal body' (pp. 4–5; for an alternative view of the historical practices of wet-nursing, see pp. 75–6 of this book). Originally deprived of their mother's breast, boys were then deprived of their wet-nurse once they were weaned, giving them 'two psychic sites of intense maternal deprivation rather than one'. Finally, the boy-child had to 'leave that femaleness behind in order to become a man, enforcing the equation of masculine identity with differentation from the mother' (pp. 4–7). It is against this psychological context, argues Adelman, that Shakespeare's plays invoke:

> the nightmare of a femaleness that can weaken and contaminate masculinity, a 'thirsty' earth-mouth that can 'gape open wide and eat him quick' (3 Henry VI, 2.3.15; Richard III, 1.2.65), a womb that is a 'bed of death', smothering its children in 'the swallowing gulf/Of dark forgetfulness and deep oblivion' (Richard III, 4.1.53; 3.7.127–8). Through this imagery of engulfment and swallowing suffocation...the womb takes on a malevolent power. (p. 4)

How far we can apply modern psychoanalytic theory to a past culture and fictional text is open to question, and I take issue with Adelman's bleak account of wet-nursing in the period. However, her attention to the note of anxiety in Shakespeare's imagery of the maternal body is extremely suggestive – particularly in the wider context of the 'range of anxieties

47

about masculinity and female power' expressed in fiction and non-fiction alike in the period (p. 3). Certainly much of the imagery of the maternal body in *Romeo and Juliet* shares a sense of threat – of contamination, engulfment, suffocation, death. The repeated allusions to the maternal body and motherhood in *Romeo and Juliet* alongside other Shakespeare plays (such as *Richard III, c.* 1592–3, and *A Midsummer Night's Dream*, written about the same time as *Romeo and Juliet, c.* 1594–5) indicate the symbolic power that maternity could wield in the period – whether as a source of danger, pleasure, or fascination.

FEMININITY, SEXUALITY, AND EFFEMINACY

> To us, in our enraptured dreams, Juliet was a true, living woman, as veritable flesh and blood as our sisters and our playmates.... Not that we imagined her to have been a well-educated English young lady, like ourselves. – Governesses forbid! We were too proper for that; – we were quite convinced of the heinous indecorum of falling in love one day, and being married clandestinely the next, without a word to papa or mamma. But, somehow, with youth's very slipshod style of argument, we managed to love Juliet all the more because we disapproved of her.[7]
>
> (Mrs. David Ogilvy, 1885)

Juliet has repeatedly posed a problem for those seeking to idealize her: as a 13-year-old girl, can her precocious sexuality, independence, and assertiveness be regarded as model, feminine behaviour? Juliet has often been recuperated as an ideal heroine on three counts: her initial modesty, her loving nature, and her rapidly developing maturity. In the nineteenth century it was commonplace for women to praise Juliet as a paragon of feminine modesty: Anna Jameson, for instance, found her 'silence and her filial deference' towards her mother in 1.3 'charming' (p. 91); Mrs Elliott admired Juliet's simplicity, naïvety, and innocence (a contrast to the precocious 'English school-girls of the present enlightened age', p. 178), while the renowned nineteenth-century actress, Helena Faucit, remarked of Juliet's confession of love in the orchard scene (2.2.85–106) that:

> Only one who knew of what a true woman is capable, in frankness, in courage, and self-surrender when her heart is possessed by a noble love, could have touched with such delicacy, such infinite

charm of mingled reserve and artless frankness, the avowal of so fervent yet so modest a love, the secret of which had been so strangely stolen from her. (pp. 118–19)

Faucit co-opts Juliet as an ideal of women in love; a demonstration of 'true' Womanhood. She attempts a balancing act between Juliet's 'fervent', frank expression of passion and the 'mingled reserve' and modesty required of women in the nineteenth century – a balance which she claims Shakespeare achieves with extraordinary 'delicacy'. But the fact that Juliet has sex aged 13 with a man she has known for little more than a day compromises this delicacy. For Faucit, as for many critics and actresses in the nineteenth century, Juliet's sexual passion could be recuperated as heroic only by appealing to her rapid maturity as a woman: initially 'girlish and immature', Faucit remarked, Juliet 'is transfigured into the heroic woman' (p. 140).

But, as we have already seen, the Elizabethan texts of *Romeo and Juliet* do not seem to point to Juliet's maturity; rather, her actions are variously described as rash, desperate, piteous and misadventured (see Ch. 2). Moreover, Juliet speaks openly about her sexual passion. Her body is open to Romeo's advances, and she enthusiastically allows him to kiss her within minutes of meeting him. 'It may be objected', commented Bulwer Lytton in 1885, 'that a modern audience would be shocked by such an unlimited and promiscuous quantity of kissing'; likewise to an Elizabethan audience Juliet's lack of restraint could have signalled a breach in feminine decorum.[8] In fact Juliet acknowledges this in the orchard scene, remarking that 'I should have been more strange' (acted with more restraint and less familiarity) but 'I am too fond' (2.2.98–102). Juliet fully reveals her feelings of sexual desire when anticipating her wedding night in her epithalamion or wedding poem (3.2.1–31; see also pp. 96–7). Indeed, Nicholas Brooke has provocatively suggested that Juliet's remark in the epithalamion, 'though I am sold,/Not yet enjoy'd' (3.2.27–8), reveals 'Juliet's discovery that in most wanting her true love with Romeo she must experience the wish to be a whore in the fullest sense' (p. 100). The epithalamion centred on the bride's sexual passion and encouraged her to express her physical desires in order for conception to take place (current medical theory maintained that women could conceive only if, like men, they emitted their

49

seed – that is, achieved an orgasm). Juliet's epithalamion, reduced to a mere four lines in the First Quarto or Q1, is more concerned with physical desire than romantic love:

> Romeo
> Leap to these arms,
>
> .   .   .   .   .
>
> Come, civil Night,
>
> .   .   .   .   .
>
> And learn me how to lose a winning match,
> Played for a pair of stainless maidenhoods.
> Hood my unmanned blood, bating in my cheeks,
> With thy black mantle, till strange love grow bold,
>
> .   .   .   .   .
>
> Give me my Romeo, and when I shall die,
> Take him and cut him out in little stars...
>
> (3.2.6–22)

Juliet is 'impatient' (3.2.30) to lose her virginity ('maidenhead'), and compares her desire – her 'blood' – with an unrestrained ('unmanned') falcon whose wings flutter wildly ('bate'). She seeks to be a 'bold' lover (3.2.15) and then looks forward to her own sexual pleasure: 'to die' was common sexual slang for orgasm. This is how Niamh Cusack, playing the part of Juliet in Bogdanov's 1986 RSC production, interpreted the line: 'my first reading of the word *die* here is the sexual one: the white of the stars, and his body in white, and the white of him ejaculating inside me'.[9] The line has curiously been emended by some editors, perhaps reticent about Juliet's precocious sexuality, to Q4's 'when *he* shall die'. As Mary Bly suggests, an Elizabethan audience would be sure to grasp the sexual double-meaning of 'die' and with it Juliet's awareness of carnal desire. But that sexual knowledge was 'a dubious virtue in light of Elizabethan conceptions of a chaste young woman's education' (explaining perhaps why 'witty heroines in Renaissance plays rarely offer immodest puns'[10]). Juliet's epithalamion, laden with sexual innuendo, is not present in Shakespeare's primary source for the play, Brooke's *Romeus*. Its addition to Q2 *Romeo and Juliet* testifies to Shakespeare's interest in the erotic nature of Juliet's passion, while its excision from Q1 points, Mary Bly argues, 'to the fact that Juliet's expression of erotic desire represented a breach of cultural expectation'.[11]

Orthodox morality in early modern England emphasized not the open expression but the confinement of unmarried women's sexual desire: thus when the moralist Juan Luis Vives issued instructions upon 'how the maid shall seek an husband' he explained 'it is not comely for a maid to desire marriage, and much less to shew herself to long therefore'.[12] Dympna Callaghan has argued that Juliet's desire is 'benign and unthreatening' (p. 84), but in my view it is shown to be unruly, leading to a rash, clandestine marriage; as Edward Snow puts it, Juliet's sexuality is not domesticated (pp. 184–5). 'There is nothing which requires more discretion', argued Richard Brathwaite in *The English Gentlewoman* (1631), 'than how to behave or carry ourselves while we are enthralled to affection'. Brathwaite's model gentlewoman should be 'never yet acquainted with a passionate *ah me*, nor a careless folding of her arms, as if the thought of a prevailing lover had wrought in her thoughts some violent distemper'.[13] But Juliet departs from such an ideal. Her opening words in the orchard scene are precisely 'Ay me!' (2.2.23–4) – a contemporary cliché for indulgent passion which Mercutio mocks in 'Cry but "Ay me!"' (2.2.10) – while her 'desperate' behaviour in threatening suicide (see 4.1.69 and 5.3.263–4) seems to manifest the 'violent distemper' Brathwaite warned women against. Brathwaite acknowledged that not all gentlewomen lived up to the ideal: some women are 'so surprised with affection as it bursts out into violent extremes; their discourse is semi-brew'd with sighs, their talk with tears'.[14] Shakespeare's Juliet corresponds more closely to Brathwaite's outline of the distempered, 'melancholy' and passionate young gentlewoman than to contemporary ideals of femininity.

There is also the question of Juliet's ethnicity: English stereotypes of Italians repeatedly emphasized their propensity for passion and sexual indulgence. Certainly appealing to ethnic difference enabled nineteenth-century critics to distance as 'foreign' what was one of the play's most problematic issues in the period: the fact of a sexually active 13-year-old girl. 'Repugnant as this may be to us,' remarked Mrs Elliott in 1885, 'we cannot dispute the fact that under Southern skies the conditions of physical and moral development are vastly different to what they are in the cold North' (p. 178). How far were such distancing strategies in operation in early modern

51

England? Certainly racial and ethnic stereotyping took place in the period, and Italians were noted for their hot blood (see 3.1.3–5) and lack of control.[15] Uncontrolled sexual passion, often attributed to the hot climate, was considered to be a national characteristic – a stereotype intensified by the demonization of Italy as the sinful centre of Roman Catholicism (see pp. 79–80). Roger Ascham, for instance, reported that on a nine-day visit to Venice he saw 'more libertie to sinne than ever I heard tell of in our noble Citie of London in nine yeare'.[16] The renowned pornographic works of Aretino (illustrated by Giulio Romano, the only artist Shakespeare mentions by name in the canon of his works; see *The Winter's Tale*, 5.2.95) confirmed an image of Italy as a place of sexual indulgence; Venetian courtesans (prostitutes) were a particular source of curiosity for English writers, and Italian sexual habits were variously commented upon with horror, humour, fear, and fascination. For an Elizabethan audience, Juliet's 'fondness' may well have signalled the sexual proclivities of a hot-blooded Italian.

Juliet also departs from contemporary ideals of female silence and submission. In the orchard scene, Juliet is far from conventionally modest or submissive towards her future husband: she dominates their discussion (Juliet has ninety-seven lines compared to Romeo's forty-six in their conversation, 2.2.49–189), asking questions (2.2.62, 79, 90, 126), and issuing orders (2.2.109, 112, 116, 138, 143–4). Moreover, Juliet takes the leading role in organizing the progress of their affair, directing their desires towards marriage, and making arrangements for it (2.2.142–70). Significantly, Juliet's parting image positions Romeo as her indulgent object – a child's pet bird ('a wanton's bird', 2.2.177), whom she controls at will:

> I would have thee gone:
> And yet no farther than a wanton's bird,
> That lets it hop a little from his hand,
> Like a poor prisoner in his twisted gyves,
> And with a silken thread plucks it back again,
> So loving-jealous of his liberty.
>
> (2.2.176–81)

Here Juliet reverses orthodox patriarchal relations by imagining herself in control of a man's movements – making him 'prisoner' to her will (she also imagines herself as a falconer and Romeo as her falcon, 2.2.158–9). And by figuring herself as the owner of a pet, Juliet reverses the conventional association of women with animals that required taming by men – a convention which Capulet shockingly employs in his characterization of Juliet as a domestic animal: 'fettle your fine joints 'gainst Thursday next....Graze you where you will, you shall not house with me' (3.5.153 and 188). Dympna Callaghan has persuasively argued that power relations within the couple are 'completely idealized' (p. 81), but I would add the qualification that, by adopting an assertive, often dominant role in her dealings with Romeo and by denying her father's authority, Juliet counters contemporary ideological imperatives for female modesty and submission; indeed, François Laroque has argued that Juliet *subverts* such imperatives (p. 18). Certainly Juliet's capacity to dominate her male lover proved troubling to Constance O'Brien in the late nineteenth century:

> in spite of [Romeo's] love and earnestness, Juliet is the leading spirit of the two; perhaps it should not be so, but she has the stronger nature and guides, where Romeo is content to worship her....From this it comes that she reverses the order of things, and asks Romeo if he means to marry her – which somehow does jar a little; she has her wits so very much about her, considering her youth and perfect inexperience.... [Romeo] is a graceful pleasant sort of lover, full of ardour and devotion; but is he quite man enough for Juliet?[17]

Far from being a simple, conventional heroine, Juliet is a complex, conflicted, and multidimensional character, whose femininity can be read in opposing ways. In my view, rather than representing a feminine ideal Juliet evokes the problematic figure of the unruly woman; the woman who challenges patriarchal dictates and social convention.

I want finally to turn to another aspect of the representation of femininity in *Romeo and Juliet*: effeminacy. Effeminacy denoted a man 'suffering' from traits normally associated in the early modern period with women – weakness ('women being the weaker vessels', 1.1.14), softness, excessive speech, tears, and sullen behaviour – and was generally claimed to be caused by sexual overindulgence in women (but could also be associated with same-sex passion between men). If Juliet departs from ideals of femininity in the period, then Romeo departs from contemporary ideals of masterful manhood by becoming, in his own words, 'effeminate' (3.1.105).[18] At the pivotal fight of the play (3.1), in a passage cut from Zeffirelli's film, Romeo cries out against his 'vile submission' to Tybalt's taunts:

> O sweet Juliet
> Thy beauty hath made me effeminate,
> And in my temper softened valour's steel!'

(3.1.104–6)

Romeo's denial of the conventional codes of aggressive, feuding, masculine honour makes him what a woman should supposedly be: submissive. Romeo perceives his 'softness' – the weakness of the manly, steel-like courage of his temper (punning on the technical tempering or strengthening of steel swords) – as effeminate, and attributes it to the effects of Juliet's beauty (a classic case of displacing blame onto the woman). But in a passage substantially cut from both Zeffirelli's 1968 film and Luhrmann's 1996 film, it is the Friar who throws most scorn on Romeo's effeminacy:

> Art thou a man? thy form cries out thou art;
> Thy tears are womanish, thy wild acts denote
> The unreasonable fury of a beast.
> Unseemly woman in a seeming man,
> And ill-beseeming beast in seeming both,
> Thou hast amazed me. By my holy order,
> I thought thy disposition better tempered.
>
> .   .   .   .
>
> Fie, fie, thou sham'st thy shape...

(3.3.108–22)

Here the Friar reveals his attachment to cultural assumptions of feminine weakness and masculine mastery. Tears and the expression of vulnerability are associated with women – real men don't cry – thus Romeo's tears become a mark of 'womanish' behaviour, 'unseemly' and shameful in a man. The Friar speaks of a contradiction between Romeo's male 'shape' and his female 'disposition', and in 'seeming both' Romeo becomes less than human, a 'beast' (the Friar's use of 'tempered' also echoes Romeo's previous qualms about his own effeminacy in 3.1.104–6). Later the Friar compares Romeo with

54

women once again: 'like a mishaved and sullen wench,/Thou pouts upon thy fortune and thy love:/Take heed, take heed, for such die miserable' (3.3.143–5). Here the Friar associates misbehaviour (mishaved) and sulkiness (sullen, pouting) with women; men, by contrast, should show more strength of purpose and adopt their rightful role of protecting women – thus he instructs Romeo to 'Go get thee to thy love as was decreed,/Ascend her chamber, hence and comfort her' (3.3.146– 7). The Nurse also compares Romeo with a woman – Juliet – when she discovers him crying in Friar Lawrence's cell: 'even so lies she,/Blubb'ring and weeping, weeping and blubb'ring./ Stand up, stand up, stand, and you be a man;/For Juliet's sake, for her sake, rise and stand' (3.3.85–9). The Nurse commands Romeo to 'be a man' by assuming mastery and supporting Juliet ('rise and stand' also bear bawdy resonances of the erect penis, as in 1.1.7–11 and 25).

The allusions to effeminacy in *Romeo and Juliet* were added by Shakespeare to his principal source – Brooke's Romeo suffers no such 'weakness' – testifying to Shakespeare's interest in the ambivalence and complexity of gender difference (something he was later to explore in plays that centre upon transvestism, such as *As You Like It*, 1599, and *Twelfth Night*, 1601). But, as Hugh Richmond observes, few twentieth-century directors 'can bear to expose Romeo to the censure that his fickleness, volatility, and homicidal moods invite us to balance against his seductive idealism' (p. 224). As a result, the text:

> is normally mutilated in the interest of suppressing its masculine reservations about a 'feminized' hero such as Charlotte Cushman epitomized, and which the actor playing Zeffirelli's own Romeo [Leonard Whiting] clearly despised.[19]

However, in the eighteenth and nineteenth centuries, Romeo was often constructed as a soft, feminized figure – as he appears in Rigaud's painting of the 'balcony scene' for *Boydell's Shakespeare Gallery* (1789), a collection of pictures that were widely exhibited, copied, and printed (see fig. 5). Hence Romeo was a part frequently played by women in the nineteenth century: his 'womanish' behaviour allowed actresses to play the part with immunity. Probably the best-known female Romeo was the American actress Charlotte Cushman, who played

5 The 'balcony scene' (2.2) by L. F. Rigaud from *Boydell's Shakespeare Gallery* (1789), a collection of pictures that were widely exhibited, copied, and printed in the late-eighteenth and nineteenth centuries. Romeo appears as a soft, feminized figure, whose features are barely distinguishable from those of Juliet.

opposite her sister as Juliet in 1845 to great acclaim (see fig. 1): 'Miss Cushman is a very dangerous young man', noted one member of the audience.[20]

This unsettling of gender stereotypes might have been made more explicit still with an all-male cast (Juliet was probably played by the boy-actor Robert Goffe). We have become so accustomed to seeing *Romeo and Juliet* acted by both men and women that it has become hard to imagine the play performed in any other way: 'Think of a boy as Juliet!... Woman's words coming from a man's lips, a man's heart – it is monstrous to think of!'[21] We cannot reconstruct how the Lord Hunsdon and the Lord Chamberlain's all-male acting companies performed *Romeo and Juliet*, but the recent production of an all-male *As You Like It* (Cheek by Jowl, 1994–5) is instructive for thinking about the range of responses an all-male production might evoke. By playing women so convincingly, Cheek by Jowl forced the audience to reconsider any preconceptions it may have had about innate differences between men and women, masculinity and femininity (the production also allowed for a homoerotic charge in the exchange of kisses between male actors). *Romeo and Juliet* could perhaps have worked in similar ways in its investigation of femininity and effeminacy. Not only does Juliet depart from orthodox models of gentlewomanly conduct, but the play exposes the fragility of gender stereotypes by showing a woman to be as strong – even less effeminate – than a man and fully capable of taking the leading role in marriage, and a man capable of 'womanish' behaviour. Far from simply reproducing orthodox ideals of gender, sexuality, and romantic love, the play seems to me to complicate those ideals in practice.

Once again, ethnicity is a possible factor in the play's characterization of gender difference. While Italian women were regarded by the English as sexually voracious, Italian men were noted for their effeminacy (which, in turn, was thought to encourage Italian men's supposed attachment to sodomy; see pp. 65–8). For an Elizabethan audience of *Romeo and Juliet*, ethnic stereotypes of male aggression, effeminacy, and female sexual passion would have been readily available as a means of interpreting the play; indeed, *Romeo and Juliet* arguably promotes these English stereotypes of Italian culture. This is how Angela Locatelli sees the play working. She argues that Romeo and

Tybalt embody the foreign, 'excessive' character: 'the unabsorbed and irreducible "other" in the Elizabethan context' (p. 73). Briefly, the 'Other' refers to a cultural or psychological construction of that which is foreign, alien, radically different; it has been a concept of particular interest to critics examining notions of cultural, ethnic, and sexual difference. Reading *Romeo and Juliet* as an exploration of an ethnic 'Other', we might say that the play distances Romeo and his feelings as both effeminate and foreign; rather than presenting an unqualified celebration of romantic love, the play instead portrays excessive Italian sexual passion. But the characterization of the exotic 'Other' usually tells more about the prejudices, concerns, anxieties, fears, and desires of the 'host' culture than it does about the 'foreign'; as Murray Levith remarks, 'Italy serves in part as metaphor for Shakespeare's England' (p. 11), and despite the play's allusions to Italian culture, it is also marked by anglicization (consider, for instance, the names of the musicians, Simon Catling, Hugh Rebeck, and James Soundpost). In my view *Romeo and Juliet* fuses Italian and English culture by projecting Elizabethan preoccupations onto a Catholic, European 'Other' – concerns such as the imposition of patriarchal authority, clandestine marriage, the control of female sexuality, the assertion of manhood, government control of aristocratic feuding and street violence. Now the play has become a well-established feature of the Veronese tourist industry and co-opted as a story of Italian lovers: thousands flock to Juliet's so-called house with its fake balcony and a bronze statue of Juliet (which reputedly brings good luck if you touch her right breast), and every year hundreds of letters are left at Juliet's so-called tomb in Verona, largely written by Italian girls about their experiences of love.[22]

MASCULINITY AND MALE BONDING

Masculinity is multifaceted in *Romeo and Juliet*. First, the play investigates the performance of manhood in different social contexts – the feud, the household, marital relations, filial relations, the church, male friendship. The 'macho' ethic of the feud has often been noted in recent criticism and performance of the play, but the aggressive (hetero)sexism encouraged by the feud is also supplemented, or complicated, by the implicit presence of homoeroticism (desire between men) in the play. Secondly, manhood is shown to be a fluid, unstable construct or performance, not properly distinct from womanhood. As a 'womanish' man (see pp. 53–5), Romeo confuses gender difference. Effeminacy threatens to undermine rigidly held distinctions between masculinity and femininity; distinctions upon which patriarchy is constructed. The play scrutinizes both the operation of contemporary stereotypes of masculinity and the patriarchal codes that depend upon them.

Mercutio reveals the extent to which male honour is bound up with mastery when he condemns Romeo's failure to stand up to Tybalt's taunts: 'O calm, dishonourable, vile submission!' (3.1.66). Submission was demanded of women in early modern England but men, on the contrary, were expected to be masterful. As Katharine Hodgkin has pointed out, mastery was 'one of the key concepts in the delineation of approved masculine virtue': gentlemen were expected to show mastery over themselves, over women, and over servants (p. 21). But Hodgkin argues that in the 1590s mastery was increasingly difficult for a gentleman to maintain: a woman on the throne (Elizabeth I) disrupted the tradition of male political mastery; women were perceived to be taking and enjoying more liberties, circumventing and undermining the authority of their fathers and husbands, and asserting their own (albeit restricted) independence; and the enormous economic shifts in late-sixteenth-century England resulted in an increasingly mobile society, in which men who were servants rose to become masters, and the numbers of so-called 'masterless men' (men without fixed employment, often homeless) increased. Mastery, concludes Hodgkin, became a growing source of anxiety for the Elizabethan gentleman.

This perhaps explains why so many of the taunts and put-downs between men in *Romeo and Juliet* centre around mastery. Consider Capulet's response to Tybalt's outburst in the masque: 'What, goodman boy, I say he shall, go to!/Am I the master here, or you? go to!...You'll make a mutiny among my guests!.../ You are a saucy boy...You are a princox, go,/Be quiet' (1.5.76–86). Capulet regards Tybalt's defiance of his authority as a form of 'mutiny', and goes on to reassert his mastery by insulting Tybalt in two ways: demeaning his age and authority by calling him a boy and a princox (a pert, conceited youth), and demeaning him socially by calling him a 'goodman boy' (a goodman was a yeoman, socially inferior to a gentleman). The episode shows how relations between men of the same feuding family are problematic; the aggression fostered by the feud cannot, in fact, be contained by it – instead it spills out into relations between uncle and nephew. Similar insults around age and status are passed between other male characters: Tybalt, for example, calls Romeo a 'Boy' (3.1.59; see also 5.3.70), while Sampson seeks to assert his social superiority over Montague's servants by remarking 'I will take the wall of any man or maid of Montague's' (1.1.10–11; as sewage ditches flowed down the middle of many streets, the pathway close to the wall was usually cleaner, safer, and consequently claimed by social superiors). In *Romeo and Juliet*, then, men do not simply express their masculinity through physical violence; they use insult to establish their mastery over others.

Gentlemen were also expected to master their own feelings: as Hodgkin notes, 'a real man was never unduly affected by passion or emotion, for his reason would keep it in check' (p. 21). But in *Romeo and Juliet* men's emotional mastery is shown repeatedly to break down. On the one hand, Romeo's 'distemper' is manifested by his 'blubb'ring and weeping' and threats to commit suicide (3.3.87 and 108) — 'desperate' behaviour which the Friar considers 'womanish' (3.3.110). Romeo's effeminacy fails to meet the demands of masterful manhood (see pp. 53–5). On the other hand Capulet brutally loses his temper with his daughter ('You are too hot', 3.5.175), while Tybalt's 'wilful choler' makes his 'flesh tremble' with anger (1.5.88–91; see also 1.1.61). *Romeo and Juliet* thus complicates the received wisdom of orthodox patriarchal ideology – that while women are subject to their feelings men are able to master their emotions, whether of anger or despair, and are therefore the 'natural' masters in society. As the 1563 *Homily of the State of Matrimony* (intended to be read aloud in every parish church) explained to husbands, women are 'prone to all weak affections and dispositions of mind more than men be ... the woman is a frail vessel and thou art therefore made the ruler and head over her'.[23] We have already seen how patriarchal authority is challenged and undermined in *Romeo and Juliet* in the context of marital, filial, and political relations (see Ch. 2). By dramatizing the breakdown of male emotional mastery, the play questions another pillar in the ideology of patriarchal authority: the assumption that men are the natural masters of women because they can control their feelings better.

The public performance of manhood in *Romeo and Juliet* is intimately bound up with aggression. Erupting at the opening, middle, and close of the play and thereby framing the love-affair, feuding violence involves all prominent young male characters (Romeo, Mercutio, Benvolio, Tybalt, Paris). Coppelia Kahn has persuasively argued that the feud provides young men with

> an activity in which they prove themselves men by phallic violence on behalf of their fathers, instead of by the courtship and sexual experimentation that would lead toward marriage and separation from the paternal house. It fosters in the sons fear and scorn of women, associating women with effeminacy and emasculation, while it links sexual intercourse with aggression and violence against women, rather than with pleasure and love.[24]

The feud fosters a culture of masculinity which is defined by violence, identified with fathers, and performed by the assertion of a man's aggressive (hetero)sexual power and prowess. The element of 'phallic violence' is brought out at the level of language, whereby talk about violence is couched in sexual imagery. The keynote is set by Sampson's and Gregory's opening exchange, in which acts of physical violence towards Montague's men become inseparable from acts of sexual violence towards Montague's women: 'I will push Montague's men from the wall, and thrust his maids to the wall' (1.1.10–16). Sampson's potentially disturbing scenario is that the rape of women becomes symbolic of (and a means of expressing) power over men. In Sampson's fantasy of male–male rivalry, women become 'trafficked' (traded) between men: that is, they become objects of exchange (in different ways, Juliet is also 'trafficked' between two men: Capulet and Paris). 'Bawdy always has a dramatic function', notes Molly Mahood, and 'here its purpose is to make explicit, at the beginning of this love tragedy, one possible relationship between man and woman: a brutal male dominance expressed in sadistic quibbles' (p. 60). I would add that Shakespeare's decision to *open* the action of the play on a note of bawdy is also dramatically significant for it undercuts the gravity of the Prologue – thereby disturbing generic expectations of tragedy – and signals the thematic importance of sex and violence in the play as a whole. The 'sexualization' of violence in the play is developed by the use of sexual innuendo to describe acts or weapons of aggression: 'tool' (1.1.28) referred both to a sword and to a penis, 'naked weapon' (1.1.29) signified both an unsheathed sword and a naked penis, while 'sword' was itself slang for penis.[25] To stand (1.1.8–10) means both to take a firm and courageous position under attack and to have an erection (and it is the sexual meaning which comes to dominate the conversation: 'me they shall feel while I am able to stand, and 'tis known I am a pretty piece of flesh', 1.1.25–6); to 'cut off' heads (1.1.22–3), as Sampson makes clear, refers both to the literal severing of heads and to the destruction of a virgin's hymen or 'maidenhead'. Other characters also link sex with violence: Romeo, for instance, draws upon conventional imagery of warfare to describe Rosaline – 'She will not stay the *siege* of loving terms,/Nor bide th'encounter of *assailing* eye' (1.1.203–4; emphasis added) – while Mercutio advises Romeo to 'be rough with love:/Prick love for pricking, and you beat love down' (1.4.27–8), a complex bawdy pun which links the act of stabbing and penetration (pricking) with the penis (prick was slang for penis), and argues that sexual desire requires 'rough' treatment ('beating down' an erection through masturbation or sexual intercourse).

But although *Romeo and Juliet* presents aggressive heterosexism and the display of 'phallic violence' as a crucial facet of masculinity, it does not condone it. As Coppelia Kahn has argued, the play is 'constantly critical of the feud as the medium through which criteria of patriarchally oriented masculinity are voiced' (p. 341). Ultimately the feud is buried, while Romeo is, quite literally, monumentalized: the golden statue Capulet promises to erect in his memory (5.3.303) marks the validation of Romeo's private manhood – his identity as a husband. The phallic violence fostered by the feud may also have been distanced by an English audience as typically Italian and elicited disapproval from an Elizabethan audience on the grounds of its 'foreign' excess. As Shakespeare's contemporary Thomas Nashe lamented, 'O Italie, the Academie of man-slaughter, the sporting place of murther, the Apothecary-shop of poyson for all Nations: how many kind of weapons hast thou invented for malice?'[26] This note of prejudicial cultural stereotyping may also have informed opinion about the most violent figure in the play and active pursuant of the feud, Tybalt. Jill Levenson has argued that, for an Elizabethan audience, xenophobia would have confirmed 'Shakespeare's broad characterization of Tybalt as a villain'. Tybalt fences in the Spanish style, identified by his habit of cutting the winds (1.1.102) and his elaborately choreographed style of duelling: 'Spanish fight... with their feet continually moving, as if they were in a dance', observed George Silver in his *Paradoxes of Defence* (1599); 'Here's my fiddlestick, here's that shall make you dance', taunts Mercutio (3.1.42; see also fig. 6).[27] The Spanish style of fencing was, however, disapproved of in Elizabethan England; moreover, anti-Spanish feeling was widespread, especially after the war against Spain of 1588. For an Elizabethan audience, aligning Tybalt with Spain would confirm his conduct and values – those of the feud – as suspect.

But feuding in *Romeo and Juliet* would also have been topical for an Elizabethan audience. Duelling, argues Joan Ozark Holmer, was 'a daily reality for the Elizabethans', and in the 1590s several English playwrights and actors (including Christopher Marlowe and Ben Jonson) were involved in life-and-death duels. She concludes that Shakespeare's portrayal of feudal violence represents 'a creative response to the problem of contemporary violence' in England.[28] Duelling was a particular problem amongst the aristocracy; proclamations against fighting in public were periodically issued by Elizabeth I, but some factions of the aristocracy continued to use street violence, particularly the duel, as a means of asserting their power. For instance in 1594, around the time of the composition of *Romeo and Juliet*, Shakespeare's patron, the third earl of Southampton, was involved in a celebrated feuding murder at Cosham (Wiltshire): he protected Sir Charles and Sir Henry Danvers after they killed a long-standing enemy, Henry Long – one of many episodes of feudal violence among the Wiltshire elite in the period. While the state intermittently sought to impose control over aristocratic violence, it did not always succeed;

63

6 'Here's my fiddlestick' (3.1.41–2). Mercutio taunts Tybalt with a phallic gesture in Michael Bogdanov's 1986 RSC production, demonstrating the provocative, aggressive use of bawdy between men in the play.

indeed the number of recorded duels jumped from five in the 1580s to nearly twenty in the 1590s. Lawrence Stone has interpreted this conflict between a feuding elite and a government seeking to curb the culture of feuding in terms of a 'crisis' in the English aristocracy which failed to adapt to the political culture of an increasingly centralized and interventionist state.[29] A similar dynamic of conflict between a feuding elite and a government unable to contain feuding violence is arguably at work in *Romeo and Juliet*; indeed, Jill Levenson argues that 'Prince Escales seems to mirror Elizabeth's conduct: temporizing and procrastination'.[30]

Romeo and Juliet is as much a play about male bonding as it is about love between the sexes. While female bonding in the play is shown to be both intimate and fragile (consider the shifting relations and 'betrayals' of trust between Juliet, her mother, and Nurse during the course of the play), bonds between men, by contrast, are defended to the death. Indeed, what Shakespeare sets in motion is a conflict between love for a wife and love between men – hence Romeo's predicament that to revenge his friend's death he has to kill his wife's cousin. Shakespeare, in his version of the story, puts considerable emphasis on the *emotional* investment between male friends – an investment made outside the remit of marital relations, and which leads Mercutio (a character largely invented by Shakespeare) to challenge Tybalt on Romeo's 'behalf' (3.1.102) and Romeo to kill Tybalt 'for Mercutio's soul' (3.1.117). In this respect, bonds between men drive the plot of the play.

Since the 1980s, social historians and literary critics alike have pointed to the presence of 'homoerotic' desire in relations between men in early modern literature and culture.[31] Homoerotic desire does not necessarily imply a sexual relationship between men – indeed, 'homosexuality' was not recognized as a distinct practice or sexual identity in the period. Rather, 'homoeroticism' (also a modern term) refers to the focusing of men's emotional energies and desires into relations between men as opposed to relations with women – desires which may become eroticized. Shakespeare's portrayal of male friendship in *Romeo and Juliet* has suggestively been viewed in such terms. When Roger Allam came to play the part of Mercutio in 1983–4 for the RSC, he drew upon his own experience of male bonding as a teenager at an English public school:

> Girls were objects of both romantic and purely sexual, fantasy; beautiful, distant, mysterious, unobtainable, and, quite simply, not there. The real vessels for emotional exchange, whether sexually expressed or not, were our own intense friendships with each other. (p. 109)

Allam saw Mercutio's friendship for Romeo as 'his closest, most passionate, and intense relationship'; thus when Romeo becomes involved with Rosaline, Mercutio feels a 'sense of loss, that Romeo was irrevocably changing', becoming 'hurt and indeed jealous of Romeo's love for Rosaline'.[32] In response, Mercutio violates the object of Romeo's love, reducing Rosaline to an inventory of her physical parts: eyes, forehead, lip, foot, leg, quivering thigh, and 'the demesnes that there adjacent lie', her genitalia (2.1.17–20). For Allam, Mercutio's insistent reduction of love for women to sex – in which women become sexual objects not emotional partners – signals Mercutio's obsession with destroying Romeo's romantic view of love between the sexes and his attempt to reclaim the bonds between men: 'Now art thou sociable, now art thou Romeo' (2.4.72–3). According to Allam, those bonds acquire an erotic charge. Mercutio first imagines Romeo with an erection: 'To raise a spirit in his mistress' circle ... letting it there stand/Till she had laid it. ... I conjure only but to raise up him' (2.1.24–9; 'raise' and 'stand' allude to erection (see also 1.1.25); 'circle' was slang for vagina). He goes on to imagine Romeo in the act of sodomy (anal intercourse): 'O, Romeo, that she were, O that she were/An open-arse and thou a pop'rin pear!' (2.1.37–8). Here, argues Allam, Mercutio reveals 'confusion around the sexuality of his relationship to Romeo, a sexuality that neither he nor Romeo allow'. Mercutio alludes to Romeo's penis on two further occasions (1.4.28 and 2.4.33–4).[33] Similarly, Joseph Porter has argued that Mercutio's emotional passion and sexual desires are directed towards men not women: 'it is as if Mercutio has a personal investment, as we say, in his friend's erection.[34] William Van Watson takes this idea a stage further: 'when Mercutio berates women for their victimized status in a male supremacist world, he actually tacitly chastises himself for his own victimized status as a repressed homosexual' (p. 250).

Van Watson is too ready, in my view, to apply modern notions of repressed homosexuality to a fictional character constructed in a past culture in which 'homosexuality' had yet to be constructed as a distinct sexual orientation or identity. But the text(s) of *Romeo and Juliet* are ambivalent about the circulation of desire between men and open to a 'homoerotic' reading. Shakespeare developed the character of Mercutio far beyond the two-dimensional courtier he appears in Brooke's *Tragicall Historye of Romeus and Juliet* (1562). In Brooke, Mercutio is a stranger to Romeo and appears only in the company of 'bashfull maydes' at the masque (p. 218, ll. 257–8); Shakespeare developed Mercutio's role extensively, placing him in the company of men – a move which testifies to Shakespeare's interest in relations between men. Emotional investment between men was not a foreign subject to Shakespeare: he explores it in other plays (such as in Antonio's 'love' for Bassanio in *The Merchant of Venice*, 1596-7) and in his *Sonnets*, probably written during the 1590s and which centre upon a passionate attachment to a young man (the well-known sonnet 18, 'Shall I compare thee to a summer's day?', was written not for a woman but for a man). Moreover, Elizabethans acknowledged the potential *ambivalence* of intimate relations between men. As Alan Bray has pointed out, not only was the sodomite a figure 'that exercised a compelling grip on the imagination of sixteenth-century England' but Elizabethans recognized that 'the public signs of a male friendship – open to all the world to see – could be read in a different and sodomitical light from the one intended.'[35] Bray points to the 'difficulty the Elizabethans had in drawing a dividing line between those gestures of closeness among men that they desired so much and those they feared', concluding that intimacy between men was 'peculiarly ambivalent' in early modern England.[36] Shakespeare's portrayal of Mercutio in *Romeo and Juliet* is poised in this 'peculiarly ambivalent' moment in the expression of male friendship and same-sex desire. In addition, Italy was stereotyped as a hotbed of sexual sin, and Italian men as especially prone to sodomy: as the learned Justice Edward Coke put it, '*bugeria* is an Italian word'.[37] Thus in Thomas Nashe's *Unfortunate Traveller*, for instance, an earl explains that young men bring from Italy only 'the art of atheisme, the art of epicurising, the art of whoring, the art of

67

poysoning, the art of Sodomitrie'.[38] Alan Bray points to English society's 'readiness, even eagerness, to recognize homosexuality in an alien context'[39] and for an Elizabethan audience the Italian setting may have helped to signal the presence of sodomy and sexual excess among the play's characters. But if Italy was demonized for its sexual licence, then so too were the London theatres. Contemporary moralists denounced the theatres for their cultivation of 'unnatural' same-sex passion, reputedly provoked by young male actors impersonating women. 'What man so ever weareth womans apparel is accursed', typically argued Philip Stubbes in *The Anatomie of Abuses* (1583) – for after plays actors and audience 'in their secret conclaves (covertly)... play the Sodomite, or worse. And these be the fruits of Playes and Interludes, for the most part'.[40] The performance of *Romeo and Juliet* by an all-male cast in an institution renowned for its sexual deviance could well have evoked, implicitly or explicitly, resonances of homoerotic passion.

Certainly the play's implicit homoeroticism has been of interest to twentieth-century producers. In Luhrmann's 1996 film, for instance, Mercutio (played by Harold Perineau) dresses up in drag for the masque, surrounds himself with beautiful young men, feels possessive towards Romeo and is clearly hurt by what he perceives to be Romeo's rejection of him in favour of a woman's love. In Perineau's performance, Mercutio's sexuality remains ambivalent. Yet the notion that *Romeo and Juliet* is solely concerned with idealized, heterosexual love persists. In 1994 an extraordinary case arose in England surrounding a headmistress's refusal to take her pupils to a Royal Ballet performance of Romeo and Juliet because it was a 'blatantly heterosexual love story'. The headmistress in question claimed that the story 'does not explore the full extent of human sexuality'; she was savagely attacked in the British tabloid press for her 'political correctness' and was threatened with suspension by Hackney Educational Authority.[41] The episode demonstrated how widespread is the notion that *Romeo and Juliet* only tells a story of heterosexual love (in fact, this is often the case in ballets of the play, which unlike Shakespeare's text(s) leave little room for ambiguity in relations between men). However, while the play has undoubtedly been *co-opted* as an icon of heterosexual love, the Elizabethan texts are more ambivalent about the expression of desire between men.

CLASS AND COMMUNITY: THE NURSE AND THE FRIAR

Shakespeare's *Romeo and Juliet* depicts a society in conflict. Opposing needs, demands, and social groups are pitted against each other, fuelling a crisis in political power as the ruler or state (represented by Prince Escales – see Ch. 2) unsuccessfully seeks to control a feuding elite (the Montagues and Capulets), and a crisis in household relations as servants (the Nurse) circumvent masters (the Capulets); additionally, the Church (represented by Friar Lawrence) comes into conflict with the 'law' (5.3.269). Indeed in David Levaux's 1991 RSC production, the play became driven not so much by passion as by political relations – above all by the troubled rule of Escales. As Peter Smith reports, Levaux's production was 'an emphatic indictment of a ruler who divides his people with threats and savagery', and ended not with 'a pair of mythologised lovers [but] took us back pessimistically, irredeemably and irrevocably to the absolute power of the state' (pp. 127–8). While 'some shall be pardon'd' by Escales others will be punished (5.3.308), and 'if the apothecary, the nurse or Lawrence are to be dealt the retribution of the state, they will have the satisfaction of knowing that it is their suffering that keeps Escales in office' (p. 127).

Amid the range of classes (or, less anachronistically, social groups) depicted in the play, Shakespeare's apothecary functions in part to highlight the inequalities between the powerful and impotent, between rich and poor. Unlike the apothecary in Brooke's *Romeus* (Shakespeare's principal source for the play), who is a corrupt villain punished by death, Shakespeare's apothecary commands sympathy through his poverty. His hunger ('Famine is in thy cheeks,/Need and oppression starveth in they eyes', 5.1.69–70) forms a striking contrast to the gastronomic plenty of the Capulet household with its banquet, dates, quinces, and baked meats (1.5.121; 4.4.1–5). Whereas Brooke uses the figure of the apothecary as a warning against evil and corrupt individuals, Shakespeare uses the episode to raise the social consequences of economic policy or 'law' ('The world is not thy friend, nor the world's law/The world affords no law to make thee rich', 5.1.73–4) and the corruption of money or 'gold', 'poison to men's souls' (5.1.80). Shakespeare's alteration to his source indicates his interest as a writer in issues of social status and inequality; indeed, Ralph Berry has argued that 'the entire action is presented through the class register'.[42] 'Class' relations in Shakespeare's *Romeo and Juliet* have interested critics on a number of counts: conflict between ruler and a feuding elite; 'class rivalry' between the Capulets and Montagues; the 'bourgeois' values of the feuding elite and/or the play as a whole; relations between masters and servants; the language of property and commerce in the play (see Ch. 4).[43] In this section I examine the Nurse in terms of her social status – looking in particular at her use of speech, and the historical practices of wet-nursing in early modern England – and the Friar as a member of a religious community who infiltrates secular social domains, and the potential anti-Catholic prejudice that he may have evoked for an Elizabethan audience.

The Nurse has traditionally been viewed in terms of her lower-class status: 'she is the one example of her class which Shakspere shows to us' in the play, argued Constance O'Brien in 1879, 'not by any means a model nurse, but a fair type of many since the time when Shakspere drew her'.[44] It is the Nurse's 'plebian' speech that marks out her low status: in 1885, for instance, Helena Faucit argued that she talks 'in the true gossiping manner of her class'.[45] The Nurse's speech is distinguished from the formal speech of the elite by her use of colloquialism ('Come Lammas-eve at night', 'broke her brow', 'by th'rood', 'by my holidam') and familiar diction (tetchy, trudge, trow, waddled, and stint). While other characters with long speeches sustain and develop an idea (witness the Friar's opening soliloquy), the Nurse's speech, printed as continuous prose in Q1, is striking for its interruptions and digressions:

> Come Lammas-eve at night shall she be fourteen.
> Susan and she – God rest all Christian souls! –
> Were of an age. Well, Susan is with God,
> She was too good for me. But as I said
> On Lammas-eve at night shall she be fourteen.

(1.3.18-22)

For Coleridge, the Nurse's rambling style of speech indicates the 'uncultivated understanding' which 'characterises the uneducated'; Stanley Wells notes, less dismissively, that the Nurse makes no pretence at relevance, and her rambles become 'a form of both self-investigation and (when conducted in public) self-revelation' which help to invoke a credible past environment for Juliet.[46]

But it is the Nurse's supposedly 'low' humour that proved especially problematic for nineteenth-century commentators: as Mrs Elliott put it in 1885, 'she is innately vulgar – as her class always have been' (p. 178). The Nurse makes nearly twenty bawdy jokes or quibbles in the play (1.3.43, 49, 52, 54, 57, 96; 1.5.116; 2.4.123, 175–6; 2.5.69, 73–5; 3.3.90; 3.5.225; 4.5.6–7, 10–11), refers frankly to her nipples and breasts (1.3.27–34), and dwells vicariously on Juliet's sex life – from her opening anecdote about Juliet saying 'Ay' to the suggestion that she would fall backwards as if to invite sexual intercourse (1.3.38–58; see fig. 7), to her eager anticipation of Romeo climbing Juliet's 'bird's nest' (slang for pubic hair, 2.5.73–5). 'It is beyond wonder', exclaimed Mrs Elliott in 1885, 'that Juliet should have escaped all taint of vulgarity, and appear the flower of refinement and gentle breeding that she does' (p. 178). The Nurse's perceived vulgarities of speech have been exorcized from texts and productions since the eighteenth century, and even as recently as the late 1980s five leading American high-school editions of *Romeo and Juliet* cut the Nurse's anecdotes about breastfeeding and Juliet's fall backwards.[47] The Nurse continues to disturb the sensibilities of what some educationalists deem appropriate for students to learn. In fact the Nurse's speech corresponds to Bakhtin's account of language use in the 'grotesque' mode (see pp. 40–1): her use of bawdy humour and frank references to the body contrasts with and undermines the discourse or 'tongue of official literature or of the ruling classes', a language governed by the hierarchy and etiquette of 'palaces, churches, institutions, and private homes' (Bakhtin p. 154). As Peter Stallybrass suggests, 'it is precisely these privileged places that the grotesque interrogates and subverts' (p. 124): the Nurse's 'vulgar' humour punctures the gravity of her social superiors. In addition, by making arrangements for Juliet's marriage the Nurse effectively usurps the parents' privilege of supervising their child's marriage, weakening Capulet's patriarchal authority (see Ch. 2).

7 'And, pretty fool, it stinted, and said "Ay"' (1.3.49) by Kenny Meadows in *The Works of Shakespeare* (1844). The illustration emphasizes the distance between the women and Lady Capulet's disapproval of the Nurse's bawdy, which seems not even to be heard by Juliet (in contrast to fig. 8). Notice that while Lady Capulet is portrayed as a relatively young woman, the Nurse's age and vulgarity are emphasized.

8   Act one, scene three: the Nurse, Lady Capulet, and Juliet enjoy each other's company and the Nurse's bawdy anecdotes in Terry Hands's 1973 RSC production. Hands stressed the intimacy and shared sexual awareness between the women (in contrast to fig. 7).

The Nurse occupies a unique position in the play: because of her lower-class status she enjoys more freedom of movement and opportunities for social exchange than any other woman portrayed in the play (see p. 37). Ralph Berry has argued that the Nurse occupies a secure and relatively powerful position in the Capulet household:

> she cannot be disciplined, and she cannot be fired. The comedy of Act 1, scene 3 rests on her tyranny over her employers and family [whereby] the Nurse is licensed to repeat her favourite recital of Juliet's precocity. It is hardly a demonstration of brutal class domination.[48]

But Capulet's treatment of the Nurse in 3.5 represents a striking contrast to the intimate scene in 1.3:

NURSE   God in heaven bless her!
    You are to blame, my lord, to rate her so.
CAPULET   And why, my Lady Wisdom? Hold your tongue,
    Good Prudence, smatter with your gossips, go.
NURSE   I speak no treason.
CAPULET   O God-i-goden!
NURSES   May not one speak?
CAPULET   Peace, you mumbling fool!
    Utter your gravity o'er a gossip's bowl,
    For here we need it not.
LADY CAPULET   You are too hot.

                                                    (3.5.168–75)

Capulet insults the Nurse by ridiculing her intelligence ('Lady Wisdom', 'you mumbling fool', 'your gravity') and demeaning her conversation or 'smatter' (meaning chat or prattle) as *gossip* – often used in early modern England as a derogatory term for interfering women and women's talk. The Nurse violates orthodox prescriptions upon women's speech in the period which demanded modesty or silence: as the moralist Juan Luis Vives advised in *The Instruction of a Christian Woman* (1529), in company a woman should 'hold her tongue demurely, and let few see her, and none at all hear her'.[49] But as Callaghan suggests, the Nurse is an unruly woman (p. 83), and her interventions with Capulet, her employer, are bold: 'I speak no treason', 'May not one speak?'

However, in 3.5 the Nurse is ultimately silenced by Capulet. After this exchange with her employer, the Nurse's role changes entirely: she no longer takes Juliet's side against Capulet. Critics have often found the Nurse's apparent 'betrayal' of Juliet and her marriage to Romeo difficult to account for. Her advice to Juliet to 'be married with the County' Paris (3.5.217) has been attributed to the Nurse's 'total want of elevated principle, or even common honesty'.[50] But the Nurse's advice to practise bigamy may also be attributed to her fear of dismissal – after all, Capulet has only just told his own daughter that she can 'hang, beg, starve, die in the streets' (3.5.192). The Nurse may enjoy comparative freedom, but she is also economically dependent upon Capulet and capable of being silenced by him. The licence that Berry observes for the Nurse should not be idealized out of hand.

How far was Shakespeare's Nurse, as Constance O'Brien argued in 1879, 'a fair type of many since the time when Shakspere drew her' (p. 143)? On the one hand, Shakespeare's Nurse is an elaboration of a classical literary type – the bawd or garrulous Nurse of Roman comedy. But wet-nursing was also commonplace in early modern England, and Shakespeare's Nurse both corresponds to and departs from contemporary patterns of wet-nursing. Many families with the available income employed wet-nurses – including merchants, lawyers, physicians, clergymen, and the gentry – but only royalty and a few members of the aristocracy employed live-in wet-nurses, and they were generally selected for their high status. Instead the usual practice was to send the child out to be nursed in the home of its wet-nurse (normally a married woman living with her family a few miles away from the employer's home) for a period of twelve to eighteen months, in which time a close relationship between nurse and child could develop. As a result, parents took particular care that their chosen wet-nurse was of good character: in 1634, for instance, Sir Simond D'Ewes was unwilling to employ a nurse of 'a proud, fretting, and wayward disposition', while Mary Verney reported to her husband that their son's wet-nurse 'lookes like a slatterne but she sayeth that if she takes the child she will have a mighty care of itt, and truly she hath [two] as fine children of her owne as ever I sawe'.[51] Although there are isolated cases of nurses who, in order to stay in employment, concealed information from parents (usually an accident, a child's illness, or their own pregnancy), most nurses were conscientious, hard-working, and responsible. As Valerie

Fildes points out, it was in the interests of wet-nurses to satisfy their employers as there was 'no guarantee that these nurses would easily find another such child to nurse, especially in relatively remote rural areas' (p. 97). In turn, children and families frequently took an interest in the welfare of their nurse later in life, paying visits, sometimes providing housing and other comforts in the nurse's old age, and remembering an old wet-nurse in a will.

Shakespeare's Nurse recalls certain features of early modern wet-nursing: the affection that might develop between nurse and child; the continued welfare of the nurse long after the initial period of wet-nursing; the possible fear of losing her job (helping to explain her 'betrayal' of Juliet in 3.5). But Shakespeare's Nurse should also be distinguished from the general pattern of wet-nursing in early modern England in that she is a live-in nurse, and of much lower status than those generally employed by the aristocracy. Shakespeare plays up the Nurse's 'low' status, her power and centrality within the household, and her capacity actively to deceive her employers. The Nurse's complicity in Juliet's secret marriage entails a level of intrigue between nurse and child that would rarely have been possible in the period. Thus Shakespeare's Nurse both evokes and departs from the historical realities of wet-nursing in early modern England.

Shakespeare's Friar poses a particular problem of interpretation: does he function as a sympathetic moral commentator acting for good and wisdom in the play, or as a more dubious figure: an inept clergyman, guilty perhaps of malpractice? Certainly Shakespeare's Friar is less sympathetic than Brooke's Friar in *Romeus* (Shakespeare's principal source for the play). As James C. Bryant notes, in Brooke's narrative the Friar is a learned 'doctor of divinitie' (1568) and a revered counsellor of the Prince, while in Shakespeare's play the Friar is reduced 'to a mere popular confessor'; in Brooke, the Friar repeatedly hesitates about the ethics of clandestine marriage ('A thousand doutes and more in thold mans hed arose', l. 597), while in Shakespeare the Friar makes 'short work' of Romeo and Juliet's marriage (3.1.35). Although Friar Lawrence performs a clandestine marriage with the intention of bringing about peace – 'to turn your households' rancour to pure love' (2.3.92) – in effect he undermines both Montague's and Capulet's patriarchal authority, flouts Catholic and Anglican church law, transgresses established social conventions surrounding marriage, and is arguably implicated in Romeo and Juliet's deaths (had he acted differently, their deaths could have been avoided). Shakespeare's Friar Lawrence is an ambivalent, problematic figure.

The Friar's defenders have argued that he is a man of peace, wisdom, and gravity: he 'knows human nature in all its varieties', argued Helena Faucit in 1885, and 'proves a most wise and comforting counsellor to Romeo'.[52] The Friar shows good humour and commonsense in his early dealings with Romeo (2.3) and responds with apparent care and affection for his young charge. He acts with good will in his attempt to bring about peace in Verona, and his calmly delivered precepts ('Wisely and slow, they stumble that run fast', 2.3.94) reputedly make him a voice of sensible gravity in the play – although Thomas Moisan has argued that the Friar merely peddles in reductive aphorisms (p. 400). The Friar's opening speech on Nature and the use and abuse of virtue and vice (2.3.1–30) has drawn particular praise (Mrs Griffith, for instance, singled it out for inclusion in *The Morality of Shakespeare's Drama Illustrated* (1775) as a 'just, ingenious, and poetical' allegory; p. 498). It is in this speech, argues Blakemore Evans, that the Friar is introduced 'as a choral voice through whom Shakespeare explains the potentiality for either good or evil in all created things' – an Orthodox Christian view that could have been shared by Catholics and Protestants alike (p. 24). The Friar functions here, in other words, as a moral commentator.

But the Friar's actions fail to live up to his words. Despite calling for moderation he is hasty in his deeds, and initiates a web of deception by marrying Juliet to Romeo without permission from her parents – and with little consideration of the social stigma attached to clandestine marriage. He instructs Juliet to deceive her parents in consenting to marry Paris (4.1.89–90, a detail added by Shakespeare to his source), resorts to the subterfuge of a sleeping potion to rescue the situation (Luhrmann's 1996 film cast a sceptical eye over the Friar's use of potions: Pete Postlethwaite played the Friar with a drug habit), and conceals Juliet's marriage to Romeo at her supposed deathbed (4.5). His most transgressive act is that of carrying out a clandestine marriage, which contravenes contemporary canon (church) law. Both Anglican and Roman Catholic canons in the period forbade the clergy from performing secret marriages, while marrying minors (children) without parental knowledge or consent was considered a serious offence and could incur a penalty of suspension from clerical duties for up to three years. Thus when Juliet takes the Friar's sleeping potion she begins to doubt his motives:

> What if it be a poison which the Friar
> Subtly hath ministered to have me dead,
> Lest in this marriage he should be dishonoured,
> Because he married me before to Romeo?'
>
> (4.3.24–7)

Juliet recognizes that the Friar's complicity in a clandestine marriage is illicit and dishonourable, and worries that the Friar has been 'subtle' – crafty or cunning – in his dealings with her (a note of suspicion not present in Brooke). An Elizabethan audience, likewise, would recognize that the Friar's complicity in a clandestine marriage breaks both canon law and contemporary social conventions of match-making and marriage. As James C. Bryant concludes, 'in view of his questionable conduct in deviating from spiritual ideals, it would seem that only a romantic and sentimental argument can exonerate Friar Laurence from obvious deceit, hypocritical posing, and prevarication' (p. 329).

But it is the Friar's actions in the final scene which have provoked most criticism: as Blakemore Evans puts it, he 'turns tail and attempts to run away, abandoning Juliet in her moment of supreme need' (p. 23). On hearing the watch, the Friar panics, exclaiming to Juliet 'Come, I'll dispose of thee / Among a sisterhood of holy nuns / Stay not to question' (5.3.156–8) – ironically echoing Capulet's efforts to 'dispose' of Juliet in marriage as though she were a piece of property ('As you be mine, I'll give you to my friend', 3.5.191). The Friar's apparent cowardice contrasts with Juliet's daring, and Juliet's frustration with him is emphasized: 'Go get thee hence, for I will not away' (5.3.160). In fact the Friar is portrayed rather differently in the final scenes of the 'rival' Elizabethan texts of the play, the First and Second Quartos (Q1 and Q2; see, Ch. 1). In Q1, the Friar is more extreme both in his cowardice and his criticism of Capulet. Q1 makes explicit the Friar's (self-centred?) fear of being arrested as an accessory for murder: 'We shall be taken, *Paris* he is slaine,/And *Romeo* dead: and if we heere be tane [taken]/ We shall be thought to be as accessarie.... I dare not stay, come, come' (p. 95). Q1 also emphasizes the Friar's disapproval of Capulet: 'her Father sought by *foule constraint*/To marrie her to Paris' (p. 97; emphasis added). Q2 softens both these aspects of the Friar to construct a less impulsive figure.

The Friar's conflicted characterization as both an orthodox moral commentator and a fallible clergyman complicit in an illicit affair is complicated still further by Shakespeare's inheritance of anticlerical and anti-Catholic traditions. An Elizabethan audience would have been familiar with the long-standing comic tradition of the friar as a butt of ribald humour (derived from medieval fabliaux, Italian novelle, and *commedia dell'arte*), in which friars were mocked for their secular foibles and human weaknesses – including deceit, hypocrisy, carnality, and depravity. As Mephistophilis puts it in Christopher Marlowe's *Dr Faustus* (*c.* 1592), 'Go, and return an old Franciscan friar;/That holy shape becomes a devil best' (3.27). Bryant argues that Shakespeare's Friar, also a Franciscan, 'becomes in some significant ways the stereotype of the sly and meddlesome friar of the medieval literary tradition' (p. 333). Certainly it is this stereotypical note that is struck in the opening address 'To the Reader' in Shakespeare's principal source for the play, Brooke's *Romeus*, explaining that the story warns against 'superstitious friers (the naturally fitte instruments of unchastitie)', 'using auriculer confession (the key of whoredome, and treason)' and 'abusyng the honorable name of lawefull mariage, to cloke the shame of stolne contractes' (ll. 213–14; in fact, Brooke's friar turns out to be a more sympathetic character than Shakespeare's Friar Lawrence). Anti-Catholic literature proliferated in the late-sixteenth century, and one of the most violently anti-Catholic plays, the anonymous *Troublesome Raigne of John, King of England* (1591), was used by Shakespeare as the basis for his play of *King John* (*c.* 1590–7), written in the same period as *Romeo and Juliet* (*c.* 1594–6). Certainly Shakespeare's portrayal of friars in his other plays is ambivalent, often emphasizing the role of subterfuge: in *Measure for Measure* (1604) Duke Vincentio adopts the disguise of a friar to carry out a series of deceitful manipulations, including substituting one woman for another in a man's bed, while Friar Francis in *Much Ado About Nothing* (*c.* 1598) devises a scheme involving a young bride feigning death. Although both friars ostensibly work for good they are devious and, in practice, tell lies.

In addition to the literary legacy of anticlericism, contemporary anti-Catholic hostility was widespread in the late-sixteenth century, particularly following the war Catholic Spain waged against England (culminating in the Armada of 1588). Roman Catholicism was associated with treason against the state and was banned in England (in practice a small minority of Catholics continued to worship in secret); the Pope and 'Popery' (as Catholicism was described) were repeatedly denounced as superstitious and corrupt, especially with the rise of Puritanism in the late-sixteenth century. Bryant points out that an Elizabethan audience watching Romeo and Juliet was 'conditioned by years of political propaganda from pulpit, stage, and published works to recognize in Roman Catholic sentiment a political threat to England and to the Reformation' (p. 322). They may have been far more sceptical of Shakespeare's Friar than a modern audience distanced from the religious conflict of the post-Reformation period.

4

Language and Ritual

PETRARCHISM AND BAWDY TALK

Language is complex and multifaceted in *Romeo and Juliet*. The play develops a striking range of different voices and linguistic registers: formal and informal; ceremonial and intimate; literary and colloquial; public and private; male and female; high- and low-status; learned and uneducated; bookish and illiterate; tragic and comic; grave and bawdy. Indeed, the play *interrogates* the use of language so that it becomes a source of enquiry in its own right ('What's in a name?', 2.2.43), not a transparent medium of communication (relating the play to others by Shakespeare with an emphasis upon language-use, such as *Two Gentlemen of Verona*, 1590–1, *Love's Labour's Lost*, 1594–5, *Hamlet*, 1600, and *Twelfth Night*, 1601). Language-use in *Romeo and Juliet* has interested critics and commentators in a number of ways: for the play's conscious 'literariness' and use of literary figures; wordplay and imagery; rhetoric, formal expression, and patterning; linguistic diversity, distinctions, and disruptions.[1] Here I want to focus upon the conflicting discourses of Petrarchism (a fashionable form of love poetry in the late-sixteenth century) and bawdy – discourses that present alternative views of love and sexuality and which continually play off and undermine each other in *Romeo and Juliet*.

In the first place, Petrarchan and bawdy discourses in *Romeo and Juliet* are inflected by distinctions of class, or more precisely the access to education that social status confers. The language of the literate and literary elite is sharply differentiated in the play from that of the unlearned – a contrast underlined by Shakespeare's detail of Capulet's illiterate servant 'I must to the learned.... I pray, sir, can you read?' (1.2.42–56; see also the

81

Nurse's comment, 'O, what learning is!', 3.3.160). Elite characters use elevated diction, sophisticated dialogue, complex imagery, learned references (such as Juliet's allusions to classical mythology in 3.2.1–3), rhetorical devices, fashionable literary styles (notably Petrarchism), and a characteristic feature of Renaissance lyric poetry, the *conceit* – an apt and ingenious comparison that invites the reader's or audience's appreciation of linguistic virtuosity and inventiveness. By contrast, the servants' use of language in the play tends to be colloquial, direct, and simply constructed. In their use of bawdy, the elite compete for verbal dexterity and wit (in the Elizabethan sense of 'intelligence'), while the servants resort to cruder, everyday sexual slang. (Such sociolinguistic contrasts are made visible in the Elizabethan texts of *Romeo and Juliet* in that the servants' dialogue is generally printed as prose while elite characters tend to speak in the more prestigious form of verse.) At another level the very images that Romeo and Juliet deploy to describe each other are appropriate to an elite, Elizabethan lifestyle. Romeo, for instance, immediately likens Juliet to 'a rich jewel in an Ethiop's ear' (an exotic, expensive object, evoking the lucrative trade of the merchant adventurer; 1.5.45), while in the orchard scene Juliet fashions Romeo as a hawk, evoking the popular pastime of gentlemen in the period, falconry (2.2.158–9). Moreover, they repeatedly use images fixing upon wealth, property, economy, and commerce – like Juliet's image of herself as a property owner ('O I have bought the mansion of love,/But not possessed it', 3.2.26–7), or the host of terms the couple use to describe each other, such as rich, dear, merchandise, sum, wealth.[2] *Romeo and Juliet* shows language-use to be inflected by social status.

One of the dominant literary motifs voiced by the elite in *Romeo and Juliet* is Petrarchism, a poetic form which became widely popular in England in the sixteenth century. Petrarchism originated from the *Rime Sparse* ('scattered rhymes') by the Italian writer Petrarch (1304–74), a sequence of sonnets to his beloved Laura first translated into English in the early sixteenth century by Sir Thomas Wyatt and Henry Howard, Earl of Surrey. Like Petrarch's *Rime Sparse*, English Petrarchism largely focused on the feelings of the male lover for his female beloved, often by celebrating an unrequited love for an idealized and unattainable woman, and typically used the sonnet form first developed by Petrarch (a fourteen-line lyric poem) and characteristic tropes – such as witty conceits (ingenious comparisons), wordplay, hyperbole (exaggeration), repetition, oxymoron (an apparent contradiction), and the 'blazon', in which the beloved's physical features were itemized and idealized. When Romeo first enters the play – melancholic, solitary, tormented – he represents an archetype of the Petrarchan lover, and launches into a string of Petrarchan oxymorons: 'O heavy lightness, serious vanity,/ Misshapen chaos of well-seeming forms,/Feather of lead, bright smoke, cold fire, sick health' (1.1.169–71). Rosaline, with 'Dian's wit' (1.1.200; Diana was the goddess of chastity), becomes the unattainable female beloved for whom Romeo swears all and, like the female beloveds of Elizabethan sonnet sequences, she never has any real presence.

Critical opinion on Romeo's use of Petrarchism is divided. On the one hand, it is argued that Romeo undergoes a transformation when he meets Juliet and matures during the course of the play, and that his bookish Petrarchan clichés give way to genuine expressions of love. Thus Blakemore Evans argues that Shakespeare 'employs Romeo's role as the lover in love with love (hence largely with himself) as a clearly realised foil to set off the new Romeo who begins to emerge after he meets Juliet and who loses his heart in a real love.'[3] Others have stressed instead the *continuity* between Romeo's love for Rosaline and Juliet – a continuity which the second Chorus seems to point to by describing Romeo's new love for Juliet in terms of the substitution of one female beloved for another: 'Now old desire doth in his death-bed lie,/And young affection gapes to be his heir' (2.1.144–5; on the use of bawdy in this Chorus see p. 88).[4] Certainly Romeo continues to speak in the Petrarchan mode throughout the play: his first exchange with Juliet is famously in sonnet form (1.5.92–105) using stock motifs of the saintly beloved and the male lover as pilgrim ('romeo' means pilgrim in Italian). In the orchard scene, as Blakemore Evans acknowledges, Romeo 'speaks in sonnet clichés' (p. 12) that recall Petrarchism's fetishistic treatment of the female beloved's body (and objects associated with it). After praising Juliet's eyes, cheek, and hand, he turns to her glove: 'O that I were a glove upon that hand,/That I might touch that cheek!' (2.2.24–5).

Before his wedding Romeo invites Juliet to join him in a poetic 'blazon', which Juliet dismisses as mere 'ornament' (2.6.31; see p. 86), and even at his deathbed Romeo invokes the standard Petrarchan motif of the female beloved's red lips and cheeks: 'beauty's ensign yet/Is crimson in thy lips and in thy cheeks' (5.3.94–5). Romeo's persistent use of Petrarchism has led James L. Calderwood to argue 'the trouble is that the old Romeo is imperfectly killed off; the ape is not really dead – too much of his Petrarchan manner and language live on in him' (p. 97). In other words, Romeo's love for Juliet is not fully distinguished from his love for Rosaline (itself a literary pose) because he continues to talk in sonnet clichés. A sceptical reading of Romeo's Petrarchism casts doubt upon the notion that Romeo matures in the play and upon the presentation of his love for Juliet as a romantic ideal.

Ann Pasternak Slater has argued rather differently that 'Petrarchism is central to the entire play – that in the love of Romeo and Juliet the empty paradoxes and hyperboles of Romeo's love for Rosaline become actual fact...his literary fantasy turns into literal reality: the beloved is a real enemy' (pp. 129–31). Thus many of the 'apparently facile tropes come true', such as Romeo's definition of love as 'A choking gall, and a preserving sweet' (1.1.185; Romeo kills himself with poison, or gall), while Romeo's use of oxymoron in the early scenes is dramatically paralleled by the sequence of oppositions and paradoxes staged by the play – such as the proximity of love and hate, or the bridal bed as grave (p. 132). In a recent deconstructionist reading of the play (that is, a reading interested in the indeterminate or slippery nature of language and sign-systems), Gayle Whittier has emphasized the 'tension between poem and flesh' in the play. She argues that 'the sonnets in *Romeo and Juliet* recollect anatomy, each verbal body reflecting the fleshly, mortal one. The hands and lips of Romeo's encounter sonnet exist both as poetic word and as visible parts of his and Juliet's flesh' (p. 40). In effect, 'the inherited Petrarchan word becomes English flesh' (p. 27) and the play enacts a slippage between poetic forms and corporeal reality; that is, the clichés of the literary form of Petrarchism (the fetishism of the beloved's features, the oxymorons or contra-dictions, the proximity of pain and pleasure) become the lived practice of Romeo and Juliet. As the play unfolds, this slippage between literature and life has tragic consequences (Romeo and Juliet's suicides). As Lloyd Davis explains, in Whittier's view 'the spirit of Petrarchism is revealed as tragically fatal and idealized romance collapses' (p. 57).

Certainly the play engages in a powerful critique of Petrarchism, and disrupts the Petrarchan modes it evokes. Mercutio soon undercuts the gravity of Romeo's Petrarchan pose:

> Now is he for the numbers that Petrarch flowed in. Laura to his lady was a kitchen wench (marry, she had a better love to berhyme her), Dido a dowdy, Cleopatra a gipsy, Helen and Hero hildings and harlots, Thisbe a grey eye or so, but not to the purpose. (2.4.34–8).

Mercutio mocks Romeo's attachment to Petrarchan form ('the numbers'), his attempt to compose poetry (Laura 'had a better love to berhyme her' in Petrarch), and his idealization of Rosaline (against which legendary beauties are deemed plain). Mercutio counters the idealizing impulse of Petrarchan discourse by repeatedly stressing the sexual, physical nature of desire. In a bawdy parody of the Petrarchan blazon, he first evokes the blazon's clichés – the catalogue of the beloved's beautiful features (Rosaline's bright eyes, high forehead, scarlet lip, fine foot, straight leg; 2.1.17–19) – and then extends the blazon to admit the beloved's genitalia and orifices: the 'demesnes' (region) that lie next to her 'quivering thigh'; her 'circle' (vagina); her 'medlars' (a small apple that was thought to resemble women's genitalia); and finally her 'open-arse' (2.2.19–38). In effect, Mercutio suggests that Romeo's love for Rosaline has more to do with sexual desire than with romance; he also hints that the poetry of romantic love may function as a sublimation of sexual desire – that verse becomes a displacement of desire. As Brecht put it, Romeo is driven by 'a bursting scrotum!... It's one of Shakespeare's great realistic strokes to notice that'.[5] Does Mercutio participate, then, in treating women merely as objects of male pleasure in his bawdy parody of the blazon? Nancy Vickers has persuasively argued that in the Petrarchan blazon women tend to be reduced to the sum of their physical parts: similarly, Rosaline tends to be commodified by Mercutio as little more than a quivering, available, 'open-arse' whose sole purpose seems to be to meet a man's physical needs and desires. But whether that commodification reveals Mercutio's latent misogyny or represents a deliberate, tactical exposure of the commodification of women in Petrarchan discourse – or a fusion of both – is left open to interpretation.

Perhaps the play's most intriguing challenges to Petrarchism, however, come from women. Before marrying Juliet, Romeo invites her to join him in a 'blazon' of their love:

> if the measure of thy joy
> Be heaped like mine, and that thy skill be more
> To blazon it, then sweeten with thy breath
> This neighbouring air...

> (2.6.24–7)

Juliet replies by rejecting the value of the 'blazon', replying that conceit (understanding) is 'more rich in matter than in words'; her concern is with 'substance', not 'ornament' (2.6.30–1). Juliet's scepticism about how far ornamental 'words' relate to substantial 'matter' is hinted at earlier in the play when she dismisses Romeo's attempts to make poetic vows of undying love in the orchard scene ('O swear not by the moon...Do not swear at all', 2.2.107–16). In effect, Juliet denies the power of Romeo's poetic discourse.

In addition, the play enacts a reversal of the usual relations of the blazon by making a man the object of a woman's blazon:

> Romeo? no, not he; though his face be better than any man's, yet his leg excels all men's, and for a hand and a foot and a body, though they be not to be talked on, yet they are past compare. (2.5.38–42)

The Nurse's prosaic blazon reduces Romeo to the sum of his bodily parts; in a similar vein, Juliet characterizes Romeo as 'sweet flesh' (3.2.81) and remarks 'What's Montague? It is nor hand nor foot,/Nor arm nor face, nor any other part/Belonging to a man' (2.2.40–2).[6] Shakespeare shows women to be both suspect of and subjects of poetic discourse, fashioning blazons for themselves and able to reproduce Petrarchan tropes (witness Juliet's skilful continuation of Romeo's pilgrim sonnet in 1.5). In *Romeo and Juliet* (as with many of Shakespeare's romantic comedies) women have a capable and often critical poetic voice, disrupting the usual relations of male agency and female passivity in Petrarchan discourse.

This disruption can also be seen at work in Lady Capulet's

curious conceit of the man-as-book, a passage unique to the Second Quarto (Q2) of the play: 'Read o'er the volume of young Paris' face,/And find delight writ there with beauty's pen', (1.3.82–95). Although this passage is often deemed over-elaborate and frequently cut from the play in production, it provides a thought-provoking foil to the use and abuse of poetic discourse among men. Amongst women, Lady Capulet fashions Paris as an object of female desire whose face can be observed at will. Crucially, Lady Capulet imagines the woman-as-reader to the man-as-book; in other words, she emphasizes female subjectivity and agency (read, find, examine, see, beautify, having him, making yourself, 1.3.82–95), while positioning a man as passive; an object to be examined (later, Juliet fashions Romeo as a 'fairly bound' book; 3.2.82–3). Lady Capulet's conceit is also intriguing for suggesting that women may read men as they read books, and for associating female subjectivity and agency with the activity of reading – as if reading represents a particularly enabling site of female empowerment. Finally Lady Capulet's conceit, with its precise attention to the material details of Elizabethan books including the binding, margins, and clasps (1.3.87–93), signals the pervasiveness of reading in the play.

Petrarchism is also disrupted in *Romeo and Juliet* with the use of bawdy innuendo by characters of all classes. Whereas Petrarchism invests in notions of idealized, romantic love, bawdy focuses upon the physical – upon sex. Bawdy talk is as vital to *Romeo and Juliet* as Petrarchan discourse – indeed, the two discourses play off against each other, presenting the reader or audience with alternative views of 'love'. Remove the extensive bawdy in *Romeo and Juliet* – as five leading American high-school editions did in the late-1980s on the grounds of indecency, or Zeffirelli's 1968 film of the grounds of obscurity – and you are left with a sanitized, sentimental, romanticized version of the play, far removed from what an Elizabethan audience would have seen or enjoyed. Similarly, readings of *Romeo and Juliet* as an icon of romantic love tend to downplay the play's bawdy. For instance, Dympna Callaghan's thesis that *Romeo and Juliet* principally promotes the ideology of romantic love and serves Protestant bourgeois views of the family, suppresses analysis of the extensive bawdy in the play – and, moreover, ignores how bawdy may function precisely to undermine the idealization of romantic love in the play. As Kent Cartwright suggests, the play 'parodies the very romance it endorses' (p. 87). In my view, Shakespeare engages with desire in complex and multifaceted ways in *Romeo and Juliet*: the play is as concerned with the crude realities of sexual desires, needs, expression, and pleasure, as it is with the workings of romantic love.

There are more sexual innuendoes in *Romeo and Juliet* than in any of Shakespeare's other plays, and for anyone attuned to Elizabethan sexual slang the play reels off one bawdy joke or quibble after another. In his classic study of *Shakespeare's Bawdy* (1948), Eric Partridge argued that Shakespeare 'took a lively, very curious interest in sex... keenly, shrewdly, penetratingly, sympathetically probing into sex, its mysteries, its mechanism, its exercise and expertise, and into its influence on life and character' (p. 7). Shakespeare entirely altered the grave, tragic tone of his principal source, Brooke's *Romeus*, by adding a bawdy register to his play. Even the Chorus engages in sexual innuendo with the effect of deflating Romeo's romantic pose. The Chorus characterizes Romeo's love for Juliet as the substitution of one object of desire for another in terms laden with sexual innuendo: 'That fair for which love groaned for and would die,/With tender Juliet matched is now not fair' (1.5.144–7). 'Groaned' carried connotations of groaning with sexual pleasure (see also 2.4.72, and Hamlet's remark to Ophelia, 'It will cost you a groaning to take off my edge', 3.2.272–5), while 'die' was slang for orgasm.

Bawdy takes different forms in *Romeo and Juliet*, ranging from the 'low', crude jokes passed between Sampson and Gregory to the 'high' wordplay with sexual innuendo performed by gentlemen, as well as the use of sexual allusion by women. We have already seen how Sampson and Gregory dwell upon the penis through the use of slang (1.1.7–29) and characterize Montague's women as sexual objects for male pleasure; indeed, Sampson articulates a fantasy of rape (see Ch. 3). However, the episode also reveals how bawdy talk is an important discursive mode between men, a way of speaking within male peer groups. Bawdy can be used as a form of provocation or insult between men: in Bogdanov's 1986 RSC production, for instance, Mercutio's taunt to Tybalt, 'Here's my fiddlestick' in 3.1.42–2), was played as a phallic gesture (see fig. 6), underlining the play's association of violence with sex. But whereas Sampson and Gregory make crude jokes using basic sexual slang, the gentlemen tend to engage in games of subtler wordplay; like Petrarchan discourse, bawdy talk is inflected by class in *Romeo and Juliet*. Consider the sophisticated exchange between Mercutio, Benvolio, and Romeo in 2.4, often cut from productions on grounds of obscurity; a passage which, argues Brian Vickers, goes 'too far' in its 'salaciousness' (p. 73):

MERCUTIO   Why, is not this better now than groaning for love? Now art thou sociable, now art thou Romeo; now art thou what thou art, by art as well as by nature, for this drivelling love is like a great natural that runs lolling up and down to hide his bauble in a hole.

BENVOLIO   Stop there, stop there.

MERCUTIO   Thou desirest me to stop in my tale against the hair.

BENVOLIO   Thou wouldst else have made thy tale large.

MERCUTIO   O thou art deceived; I would have made it short, for I was come to the whole depth of my tale, and meant indeed to occupy the argument no longer.

ROMEO   Here's goodly gear!

(2.4.72–82)

The passage plays upon a series of bawdy quibbles: groaning (evoking groans of sexual pleasure and echoing the Chorus's innuendo in 1.5.146); bauble (a fool's short stick, or penis); hole (quibbling on vagina); stop in (cease, or stuff in; penetrate); tale (story, or genitalia); against the hair ('against the grain', but quibbling on pubic hair); large (long, or erect); short (quibbling on flaccid); come to the whole depth of my tale (reached the end of my story, or achieved orgasm); occupy (continue in, or have intercourse with); argument (quibbling on vagina); gear (nonsense, or genitalia). Although Mercutio dominates the conversation, all three men participate in the production of sexual innuendo; here bawdy talk becomes a game played between men. We might see this game as primarily linguistic – a friendly competition for the cleverest continuation of sexual innuendo (ultimately reflecting, of course, on the author's linguistic skills) – and/or as an assertion of masculinity and male sexual prowess. Certainly Mercutio suggests that bawdy talk is a defining feature of male 'sociable' identity: only when Romeo joins him in jokes about genitalia, sexual intercourse, venereal disease, and prostitution (2.4.40-55 and 61–71), does Mercutio consider Romeo 'sociable' and truly himself: 'now art thou Romeo'. Romeo's identity, so Mercutio implies, is bound up in his ability and willingness to play the game of bawdy talk between gentlemen.

Bawdy talk is not part of female 'sociable' identity in the same way, and in this respect *Romeo and Juliet* distinguishes between men's and women's use of sexual innuendo. The Nurse, as we have already seen (Ch. 3), makes nearly twenty bawdy allusions in the play, ranging from everyday sexual slang to jokes about sex and conception and her vicarious pleasure in imagining Juliet's sexual encounters. Although, like her fellow servants Sampson and Gregory, the Nurse adopts the 'low' bawdy register, her humour takes a very different vein. She does not associate sex with violence but rather with mutual pleasure, moreover, she emphasizes women as the subject (not objects) of sexual pleasure – as in her allusion to Juliet's 'delight' when making love with Romeo (2.5.74), or her remark that Juliet has 'no use of him' once he is banished ('use' carried sexual connotations, 3.5.225). And by contrast to much of the bawdy talk of male servants and gentlemen, the focus of the Nurse's bawdy is rarely upon male or female genitalia but rather upon the *act* of making love – as in her comments about Juliet falling backwards, bearing the burden, growing bigger, using Romeo, and resting little with Paris (1.3.43, 2.5.75, 1.3.96, 3.5.225, 4.5.7). The Nurse's bawdy functions on several levels: it calls attention to distinctions between men and women's use of bawdy (notice how the Nurse is offended by Mercutio's bawdy remarks: 'I am none of his flirt-gills', 2.4.127); it raises differences in the use of sexual innuendo by low-status and high-status women (Lady Capulet makes no bawdy jokes and seeks to silence the Nurse's in 1.3, while Juliet's sexual innuendoes tend to be less crude or colloquial); it counters the romantic idealization of Juliet – instead the Nurse emphasizes her sexuality and the physicality of her desire – and consequently it challenges, even undermines, the idealization of romantic love in the play.

Although women do not engage in bawdy talk to the same extent as men, *Romeo and Juliet* arguably shows women enjoying sexual innuendo together out of the company of men – as Mercutio seems to suggest in the line 'that king of fruit/As maids calls medlars, when they laugh alone' (2.2.35–6; alternatively, Mercutio articulates a fantasy of women talking about sex). Terry Hands's 1973 RSC production explored the potential for women's shared enjoyment of sexual innuendo (see fig. 8):

> as the Nurse launched into her lengthy reminiscence of Juliet's infancy, mother and daughter sat side by side, stifling laughter which burst forth at the Nurse's bawdy joke ['Thou wilt fall backwards when thou has more wit', 1.3.43]. The laughter suggested the shared awareness of two adult women, unembarrassed by their sexuality and amused by the servant who was playing to her audience.[7]

Similarly in Rakoff's BBC television production of *Romeo and Juliet* (1978), Lady Capulet 'enjoys' the Nurse's anecdote 'with graciousness and intelligent humour' (Davies, p. 160). But this 'shared awareness' of sexual innuendo among women proved problematic for nineteenth-century commentators who sought a discreet, modest, and sexually innocent Juliet. In 1885, for instance, Mrs. Elliott suggested that Juliet probably did not understand the Nurse's crude remarks (p. 178), while the alleged distance between the Nurse, Juliet, Lady Capulet, and their use of bawdy is emphasized in Kenny Meadows's illustration to the Nurse's anecdote about Juliet falling backwards in Mary Cowden Clarke's 1862 edition of *Romeo and Juliet* (fig. 7): Lady Capulet shoots a disapproving look at the Nurse, while Juliet has her face turned completely away from her, as if hardly listening. But the play's suggestion of women's shared awareness of sexuality, revealed especially by Juliet's and the Nurse's use of sexual innuendo, is particularly interesting given early modern restrictions upon women's speech. Juliet's frank admission of her sexual passion in her epithalamion or wedding poem (see Ch. 3), for instance, does not meet the contemporary ideal of the modest and virginal adolescent girl. Similarly, Juliet and the Nurse's engagement in bawdy talk runs against contemporary orthodox prescriptions for women's chaste speech; *Romeo and Juliet* counters received ideology of feminine silence around sex (see Ch. 3). As Mary Bly argues, 'the woman's revelation of desire may strengthen the audience's belief in the romantic relationship being staged, but it also violates a fundamental convention regarding the behaviour of a marriageable young female' (p. 108).

The affirmation or denial of a 'shared awareness' of sexual innuendo among women in the play helps to reveal how bawdy impinges upon notions of a character's identity. The Nurse's 'vulgar' humour helps signal her lower-class status (though, as Mercutio demonstrates, the elite also engage in bawdy), while participating in bawdy talk is shown to be a facet of 'sociable' male identity (both on the part of the elite and their servants). And if we acknowledge Juliet's engagement in sexual innuendo, then we have to admit her identity as a 13-year-old girl with a sexually active imagination (she is a creature of flesh, not just romance). But bawdy also works in *Romeo and Juliet* to demystify and undermine the idealization of romantic love: it mocks the gravity and profundity espoused in discourses of romantic love (especially Petrarchism); it counters the emotional with the physical, the mind with the body, and tends to reduce love to sex. In so doing, bawdy talk in *Romeo and Juliet* corresponds to Bakhtin's notion of the grotesque body with its mocking 'degradation' of 'high' culture (see p. 40):

> [Degradation] is the lowering of all that is high, spiritual, ideal, abstract; it is a transfer to the material level . . . To degrade [means] to concern oneself with the lower stratum of the body, the life of the belly and the reproductive organs; it therefore relates to acts of defecation and copulation, conception, pregnancy and birth.

Bawdy can work to 'degrade' romantic ideals and expose sexuality; an exposure which has discomforted generations of producers, performers, editors, and critics of the play, as signalled by the alterations and emendments that the play has undergone over four centuries. *Romeo and Juliet* is much more than an exercise in the idealization of romantic love: it explores conflicted discourses and experiences of romantic and sexual desire. Ultimately, in my view, the play does not so much promote romantic love as *complicate* it, and bawdy talk participates in that complication.

THE WORK OF RITUAL: BETROTHAL, BRIDAL BEDS, AND DEATHBEDS

> Both in its social and psychological consequences, ritual confirms and strengthens social identity and people's sense of social location:

it is an important means through which people experience community.

(Cohen, p. 50)

Romeo and Juliet is shaped by ritual. On the one hand, religion provides a source of ritual behaviour and imagery in the play. Luhrmann's 1996 film emphasized the role of Catholicism in the play by showing Catholic rituals and spaces (confession, prayer, worship, offerings, altars, shrines, church, the Madonna) and using the extraordinary modern-gothic church of the Immaculate Heart of Mary (Mexico City) as a 'set'. But the play is also heavily invested in 'secular' rituals – ranging from the ritualized violence of the feud to the formalities of the masque (1.5); from courtship to consummation; from the bridal bed to the deathbed; from celebration to mourning. Furthermore, the play dramatizes two key rites of passage in early modern English society: marriage and death. in *Romeo and Juliet*, participation in public rituals, as Anthony Cohen suggests, works to confirm and strengthen 'social identity and people's sense of social location': feuding violence, for instance, both intensifies partisan identification with the family and provides young men with an arena for the performance of manhood (see Ch. 3); the ritualized mourning of the 'lamentation scene' (4.5) intensifies Capulet's and Lady Capulet's identities as parents (hence the repeated allusions to their parenthood; my child, my daughter, one poor and loving child, O child, O child!, my child, my child; 4.5.19, 39, 46, 62–4) and unites the Capulet household, masters and servants, parents and wet-nurse, in grief. But *Romeo and Juliet* also dramatizes the *disruption* of rituals that would normally be acted in public in early modern England by showing their enactment in private, 'untalked of and unseen' (3.2.7). This disruption points to social *dislocation* in Shakespeare's Verona: attending to ritual behaviour in *Romeo and Juliet* against the historical context of Elizabethan culture can reveal not only the construction but the fragmentation of community in the play.

The 'orchard' or 'balcony' scene has often been regarded as a portrayal of a spontaneous outpouring of romantic love. But this view needs some qualification, for Romeo and Juliet make their protestations of love within a ritual framework of betrothal, responding to formal codes of behaviour in Elizabethan England. Romeo and Juliet exchange vows, oaths, and verbal contracts, and look forward to their marriage rites. Juliet's concern is with Romeo's pledged commitment of love – 'If thou dost love, pronounce it faithfully' (2.2.94) – evoking the contemporary practice of formally pronouncing out loud a promise to marry as the first step of betrothal. She uses legal terminology when expressing doubts about their betrothal: 'Although I joy in thee,/I have no joy of this *contract* tonight' (2.2.116–17; emphasis added). As T. E. explained in *The Law's Resolutions of Womens' Rights* (1632) betrothal 'hath an inception first and then an orderly proceeding. The first beginning of marriage (as in respect of *contract* and that which law taketh hold on) is when wedlock by words in the future tense is promised and *vowed*'.[8] Romeo then calls for 'th'exchange of thy love's faithful vow for mine' (2.2.127); later, Juliet confirms their 'contract' by requesting instructions as to 'where and what time thou wilt perform the *rite*' of marriage (2.2.146; emphasis added).

Jill Colaco has outlined another ritual context for the balcony scene: the Night Visit, a folklore tradition rooted in oral culture. She points to the plethora of contemporary ballads with plotlines similar to *Romeo and Juliet*: a woman crossing feud lines or family rules by taking a lover; a woman choosing between an official suitor and a true sweetheart; the double death of lovers who will not be parted; a mock death designed to bring two lovers together (in the seventeenth-century ballad of 'The Gay Goshawk', for instance, a woman takes a sleeping potion, her family make elaborate preparations for her funeral, and she awakes in secret to claim her lover; p. 152). Night Visit ballads also involve a man courting a woman at a window, who later admits her sweetheart into the house where they secretly make love; 'the exchange is a kind of ritual', Colaco explains (p. 141). Colaco argues that the balcony scene follows the pattern of the Night Visit: not only does Juliet appear at a window ('what light through yonder window breaks?', 2.2.2) but she 'is never out of tune with the mood of the Night Visit, even when she talks of marriage' (the ballads tend to involve sex before marriage); the scene evokes the language of Night Visit ballads (Romeo's 'My true-love passion', for instance, 'vividly employs the familiar terminology of ballad'), and, as the scene draws to a close, 'Juliet's repeated recalling of Romeo traces the old Night Visit pattern of the woman's last-minute recalling of the suitor she had dismissed' (pp. 145–6). The evocation of the Night Visit tradition in the balcony scene has some intriguing implications. First, it serves to connect *Romeo and Juliet* with both literary and oral, elite and popular culture: the play, 'with all its sophistication, draws on a popular tradition in keeping with the story's folklore origins', and Shakespeare, Colaco argues, was 'inviting his audience to associate his lovers' words with the language and ways of folksong' (pp. 138 and 155). Secondly, the parallels between the balcony scene and the Night Visit tradition associate Romeo and Juliet's 'contract' with illicit action: although Night Visit ballads tend to involve sex before marriage, Romeo and Juliet's married life begins 'more like the private betrothal meeting in which Night Visit songs probably originated than like the consummation of a legal and church-blessed union' (p. 153). For an Elizabethan audience, then, the evocation of the Night Visit tradition would work to heighten the clandestine nature of Romeo and Juliet's affair and marriage (see also Ch. 2).

Later, the play stages the disruption of public rituals surrounding the bridal bed and deathbed. The bed is given prominence on stage: precise stage directions in Q1 emphasize the material presence of Juliet's bed ('She falls upon her bed, within the curtains'; 'Nurse Draws back the curtains', Q1, 4.3.58 and 4.5.11), and Elizabethan staging practice may have visually emphasized the Death-as-Bridegroom motif by using the same stage space (probably the tiring-house) for Juliet's bridal bed and tomb. Traditionally the play's repeated reference to the bridal bed and deathbed have been viewed in terms of the Death-as Bridegroom motif, expressed in lines such as 'My grave is like to be my wedding bed' (1.5.134); 'I'll to my wedding bed,/And death, not Romeo, take my maidenhead' (3.2.136–7); 'make the bridal bed/In that dim monument where Tybalt lies' (3.5.200–1; see also 3.5.140, 4.5.38–9, 5.3.102–5).[9] But these insistent allusions in the play also signal contemporary rituals surrounding the wedding- and deathbed, and an Elizabethan audience would have been keenly aware of the rites of passage that are both evoked and disrupted in the play. (In fact, for many men and women the wedding bed could quite literally have been their deathbed: beds were kept for years, classed as family heirlooms and 'unmovables' – furniture too bulky to be moved – and the bed in which a couple consummated their marriage could well have lasted until their deaths.)

Juliet's bridal bed represents the *disruption* of public rituals marking marriage in early modern England. The 'bedding ceremony' was the culmination of a series of marriage rites and celebrations: it was an elaborate public preparation of the couple's sexual consummation of their marriage.[10] The bed-chamber was strewn with flowers and herbs – echoed in Capulet's lament that 'Our bridal flowers serve for a buried corse' and the Q1 stage direction 'They all, but the Nurse and the Musicians, go forth, casting rosemary on her, and shutting the curtains' (4.5.89 and 95; rosemary, for remembrance, was given at weddings). The specially dressed bridal bed was formally blessed; the wedding party were invited to enter the freshly decorated bedchamber, and share a drink with the bride and groom who were already in bed; the bride might be sewn into the sheet, and games were played such as 'flinging the hose' (in which the bride, groom, best man, and bridesmaid threw stockings at each other on the bridal bed). Finally the wedding party kissed the bride goodnight and left the couple to consummate their marriage. The publicity of the bedding ceremony, which continued late into the seventeenth century, is confirmed by Samuel Pepys's account of an especially 'modest' wedding he attended in 1665. Pepys reports that he:

> got into the bridegroom's chamber while he undressed himself, and there was very merry – till he was called to the bride's chamber and into bed they went. I kissed the bride in bed, and so the curtaines drawne with the greatest gravity that could be, and so good-night.[11]

An elite gentlewoman could normally expect a range of publicly witnessed rituals at her bridal bed – unless she was involved, like Juliet, in a clandestine marriage. Juliet's 'wedding bed' (3.2.136) is shrouded in secrecy. Far from being accompanied to Juliet's bedchamber by the wedding guests, Romeo has to make a surreptitious entry by rope ladder (3.2.132–4), and their 'amorous rites' must remain 'untalked of and unseen' (3.2.7). The very secrecy surrounding Juliet's bridal bed denotes the transgression of her clandestine marriage.

The disruption of contemporary wedding rituals also takes place with the recital of Juliet's epithalamion or wedding poem (3.2.1–31; see also pp. 49–50). As George Puttenham explained in

The Arte of English Poesie (1589), the epithalamion or 'bedding ballad' was sung 'very sweetely by Musitians at the chamber dore of the Bridegroome and Bride...at the bedding of the bride'; it both helped to mask 'the shreeking & outcry of the young damosell feeling the first forces of her stiffe & rigorous young man' and sought to encourage 'the bride so lustely to satisfie her husbandes love...to animate new appeties with cherefull wordes'.[12] A classical poetic form, the epithalamion was revived in the late-sixteenth century to become part of the public ceremony of an elite wedding – many were written on the occasion of aristocratic weddings, such as Edmund Spenser's *Spousall Verse...in Honour of the Double marriage of the two Honorable and vertuous Ladies, the Ladie Elizabeth and the Ladie Katherine Somerset* (1596). Juliet's epithalamion shares many of the characteristics of contemporary epithalamia: the use of classical allusion (Phoebus' lodging, Phaeton); the appeal to a benevolent external force to aid the bride ('Come civil Night, and learn me how to lose a winning match,/Played for a pair of stainless maidenhoods'); the emphasis upon the bride's sexuality ('Hood my unmanned blood, bating in my cheeks'); the anticipation of sexual consummation ('and when I shall die...'). But Juliet's epithalamion crucially differs from Elizabethan convention in that it is spoken by herself, alone. She appropriates a role usually reserved for men (normally the composers and performers of 'bedding ballads'), and she performs that role in private.

A similar disruption of public rituals and rites of passage takes place over Romeo and Juliet's deathbed. Death took place in the home, not the hospital, in early modern England: in their final hours the dying were comforted in bed by close friends, relatives, and possibly a clergyman; after death the body was laid upon the bed for people to pay their last respects, and both bed and bedchamber were draped in mourning cloth. By contrast, Romeo and Juliet die alone, without the comfort of family and friends, and out of their beds; once again, a ritual that is normally publicly enacted or witnessed within the home is disrupted. *Romeo and Juliet* concludes with another allusion to contemporary rituals surrounding death: the erection of funerary monuments. Montague's promise to 'raise [Juliet's] statue in pure gold' and Capulet's response to erect a statue of

Romeo (5.3.299–304) has been regarded as a trite commemorative gesture: as Susan Snyder argues, it 'suggests vulgar show...an inauspicious beginning for a new era of peace'.[13] But the father's gesture can also be viewed as an enactment of contemporary practices of honouring the dead, and as a restoration of a public ritual after the disruption of rites surrounding the bridal bed and deathbed. Statues to the dead, often painted in garish colours and gold leaf, proliferated in the late-sixteenth century; some can still be seen today in English parish churches, including Shakespeare's own funeral monument in the Holy Trinity Church of Stratford-upon-Avon.

I want to turn finally to the rituals of reconciliation that conclude the play. The final scene of *Romeo and Juliet* has caused directors problems: Romeo and Juliet die little over half-way through the scene, and the 140 lines that follow their deaths can seem something of an anticlimax. Not only does the Friar's 'brief' speech recapitulate events that the audience has already seen, but as Peter Holding notes 'modern audiences find the public demonstrations of grief that end the play rather hard to accept: we seem to demand spontaneous emotion and we are suspicious of any reconciliation that is expressed through the medium of ritual or formal rhetoric' (p. 74). Zeffirelli's response was to cut most of the scene following Juliet's death, retaining only the last fifteen lines; likewise Luhrmann's 1996 film cuts and compresses the last 140 lines of the scene. In Michael Bogdanov's 1986 RSC production, Juliet's death was followed by a brief blackout and then the curtains opened to reveal a 'reconciliation' blatantly posed as a publicity stunt. Two golden statues of Romeo and Juliet were ceremoniously unveiled in front of television cameras; the remaining characters lined up to have their pictures taken by the *paparazzi* (the Nurse holding the all-important rope ladder), and the Prince exited through the audience pursued by the media. Niamh Cusack, who played Juliet in the production, argues that treating the ending of the play in this way:

> is to refuse to soften the play, as Shakespeare rather tends to, in its finale. It seems to me to make the play much more real for the audience.... We also cut Friar Laurence's long recapitulation, again with the idea of not allowing the audience to find comfort in distancing themselves from the situation through a long passage of narrative. (p. 129)

But, as Peter Holding has argued, cutting the final scene in this way, although 'theatrically effective', marks a 'refusal to confront the play's final public rituals' and denies the 'complicated mix of emotions' operating in the final scene (pp. 35 and 51).

The rhetorical effects of the final 140 lines of the scene can in fact be remarkably powerful on stage. Instead of 'softening' the audience from the tragic suicides, the graphic descriptions of the bleeding bodies force the audience to confront Romeo and Juliet's death: 'the ground is bloody', 'Juliet bleeding, warm, and newly dead', 'Romeo dead, and Juliet, dead before,/Warm and new killed', 'O wife, look how our daughter bleeds!' (5.3.172, 175, 196–7, 202; compare the Nurse's account of Tybalt's 'gore' in 3.2.56). Played with care such lines can provoke, not deaden, the audience's feelings and evoke more horror than the actual suicides themselves. Similarly, instead of 'distancing' the audience from the tragedy on stage, the Friar's recapitulation of events demands that the audience relive and reconsider what it has just witnessed; it can be used to heighten not diminish the tragic effect. The Friar calls the audience's attention to the lovers' dead bodies and past histories ('Romeo, there dead...And she, there dead', 5.3.231–2); he persistently asks the audience to confront the tragedy of their deaths as well as those of Paris and Tybalt (5.3.234–64), and adds a note of pathos by commemorating Romeo and Juliet's fidelity and privileging their identities as husband and wife ('husband to that Juliet', 'Romeo's faithful wife', 5.3.231–2). Simon Parry's 1996 production of the play (New End Theatre, London) recognized the strengths of the scene's rhetorical effects, and the Friar played by Andrew Potter drew tears from the audience. The final lines of *Romeo and Juliet* need not necessarily 'soften' the play.

Shakespeare chose to end his play not with the disrupted rituals of the deathbed – the private suicides of Romeo and Juliet – but with the public display of grief, reprimand, and reconciliation (though in David Levaux's 1991 RSC production, the keynote was less reconciliation than the imposition of absolute power by Escales; see Ch. 2). Romeo and Juliet are acknowledged in their identities as husband and wife, and with the promise of a funerary monument the private becomes reincorporated into the public body. This is reiterated in the Prince's final instruction 'to have more talk of these sad things'

(5.3.307): what had previously been 'untalked of and unseen' now becomes spoken in the public domain. As Peter Holding suggests, the play ends with an acknowledgement of the interrelatedness between public and private domains, for in the private suicides of Romeo and Juliet 'All are punished' (5.3.295); the tragedy is not contained by the deaths of the young couple but spills over to claim other men and women, and will become the matter for public 'talk' (5.3.307).

But this acknowledgement does not necessarily constitute a 'closure'. While a historically sensitive reading of the play must admit the importance of the public rituals of grief, reprimand, and reconciliation enacted in the final scene and the reincorporation of the private into the public body, the text is left open as to how easily or successfully this consensus is achieved. Even following the Elizabethan texts to the letter, a director can choose at the play's conclusion, for instance, to have all the characters remain on stage, exit together (as a show of unity), or leave the stage through separate exits (underlining the continued distance between the feuding families). Nor is the reconciliation enacted by the final scene necessarily easily achieved. Shakespeare takes pains to bring every remaining character on stage in 5.3 and the text(s) allow for considerable complexity in their interaction. As well as the more familar notes of grief and reconciliation, the scene can encompass anger, revulsion, disappointment, embarrassment, humiliation, inadequacy, or despair; John Woodvine's Capulet in Trevor Nunn's 1976 RSC production kicked Romeo's corpse in the tomb and brandished a dagger at the Friar. Lines such as the Prince's 'We still have known thee for a holy man' (5.3.270) or Capulet's 'no more/Can I demand' (5.3.297–8) can be made to bristle with tension. Furthermore, the final reconciliations of the play are hedged with ironies: the gold statues with which Capulet and Montague symbolize their reconciliation, while evoking contemporary funeral monuments, can also disturbingly echo Romeo's previous attack on gold as 'poison to men's souls' (5.1.80), and Capulet and Montague's exchange (5.3.296–304) arguably carries a note of competitiveness. Both fathers, Susan Snyder suggests, 'speak the language of commercial rivalry as they strive not to be outdone in conspicuous display'.[14]

The Elizabethan texts of *Romeo and Juliet* remain ambivalent, open to conflicting interpretations even in their closing lines. The final reconciliations do not guarantee good social relations in 'Verona', or even lay to rest the many social tensions that the play has already explored – such as the performance of masculinity; crisis in patriarchal authority; the expression of female sexuality; troubled relations between governors and citizens, families and rivals, parents and children, husbands and wives, masters and servants, and peer groups. *Romeo and Juliet* is much more than its ending, and the play will continue to provoke different interpretations and new readings.

Notes

Note: For full references to frequently cited texts, please consult the Select Bibliography.

CHAPTER 1. WHICH *ROMEO AND JULIET*?

1 See G. Blakemore Evans (ed.), *Romeo and Juliet*, The New Cambridge Shakespeare (1984; Cambridge: Cambridge University Press, 1992), 36.

2 Jill L. Levenson, *Shakespeare in Performance: Romeo and Juliet* (Manchester: Manchester University Press, 1987), 110.

3 See James Andreas, 'The Neutering of *Romeo and Juliet*', in Robert P. Merriz and Nicholas Ranson (eds.), *Ideological Approaches to Shakespeare: The Practice of Theory* (Lampeter: Edwin Mellin Press, 1992), 229–42; and Rex Gibson, '"O, what learning is!" Pedagogy and the Afterlife of *Romeo and Juliet*', in *Shakespeare Survey 49* (1996), 141–51.

4 On the First Quarto of *Romeo and Juliet*, see Alan C. Dessen, 'Q1 *Romeo and Juliet* and Elizabethan Theatrical Vocabulary', in Jay L. Halio (ed.), *Shakespeare's 'Romeo and Juliet': Texts, Contexts, and Interpretation* (Newark and London: Associated University Press, 1995), 107–22; Jay L. Halio, 'Handy-Dandy: Q1/Q2 *Romeo and Juliet*', in Halio, *Shakespeare's 'Romeo and Juliet'*, 123–50; David Farley-Hills, 'The "Bad" Quarto of *Romeo and Juliet*', *Shakespeare Survey 49* (1996), 27–44; Graham Holderness, *Romeo and Juliet*, Penguin Critical Studies (Harmondsworth: Penguin, 1990), 46–53; Steven Urkowitz, 'Five Women Eleven Ways: Changing Images of Shakespearean Character in the Earliest Texts', in Werner Habicht, D. J. Palmer, and Roger Pringle (eds.), *Images of Shakespeare* (London and Toronto: University of Delaware Press, 1986), 292–304; and Cedric Watts, *Romeo and Juliet*, Harvester New Critical Introductions to Shakespeare (London: Harvester, 1991), 3–12.

5 See Blakemore Evans, *Romeo and Juliet*, 206–7.

6 Holderness, *Romeo and Juliet, 48*.

7 Leah Marcus, 'Levelling Shakespeare: Local Customs and Local

Texts', in *Shakespeare Quarterly*, 42:2 (summer 1991), 169–78 (p. 168). On textual criticism see, for instance, Graham Holderness, *Romeo and Juliet*, and '"My grave is like to be my wedding bed": Stage, Text and Performance', in Linda Cookson and Bryan Loughrey (eds.), *Romeo and Juliet*, Longman Critical Essays (Harlow: Longman, 1991), 19–28; Bryan Loughrey, Graham Holderness and Andrew Murphy, '"What's the matter?" Shakespeare and Textual Theory', in *Textual Practice*, 9:1 (1995), 93–115; and Gary Taylor's General Introduction to Stanley Wells and Gary Taylor, *William Shakespeare: A Textual Companion* (Oxford: Clarendon Press, 1987).

CHAPTER 2. FAMILY DYNAMICS

1 For *Romeo and Juliet* as a tragedy of character, see Dickey's famous attack on the lovers' immaturity in Franklin M. Dickey, *Not Wisely But Too Well: Shakespeare's Love Tragedies* (San Marino, CA: Huntington Library, 1957); and see also John F. Andrews, 'Falling in Love', in John F. Andrews (ed.), *Romeo and Juliet: Critical Essays* (London: Garland Publishing Inc., 1993); Blakemore Evans (ed.), *Romeo and Juliet*; Peter Holding, *Romeo and Juliet: Text and Performance* (London: Macmillan, 1992); Joan Ozark Holmer, 'The Poetics of Paradox: Shakespeare's versus Zeffirelli's Cultures of Violence', *Shakespeare Survey 49* (1996), 163–79; Hugh M. Richmond, 'Peter Quince Directs *Romeo and Juliet*', in Marvin and Ruth Thompson (eds.), *Shakespeare and the Sense of Performance* (London: Associated Press, 1989), 219–27; R. S. White, 'Romeo and Juliet', in Stanley Wells (ed.), *Shakespeare: A Bibliographical Guide* (Oxford: Clarendon Press, 1990), 188–200.

On the play as a tragedy of fate, see Lloyd Davis, '"Death-Marked Love": Desire and Presence in *Romeo and Juliet*', in *Shakespeare Survey 49* (1996), 57–67; Helena Faucit, *On Some of Shakespeare's Female Characters* (Edinburgh: Blackwood and Sons, 1885; 7th edn. 1904); Anna Jameson, *Shakespeare's Heroines* (London, 1897); Levenson, *Shakespeare in Performance*.

On the play as a tragedy of circumstance, see Coppelia Kahn, 'Coming of Age in Verona', *Modern Language Studies*, 8:1 (spring 1978), 171–93, repr. in her book *Man's Estate: Male Identity in Shakespeare*, 1981, and in John F. Andrews (ed.), *Romeo and Juliet: Critical Essays* (London: Garland Publishing, Inc., 1993), 337–58; Susan Snyder, '*Romeo and Juliet*: Comedy into Tragedy', *Essays in Criticism*, 20 (1970), 391–402, repr. in Andrews, *Romeo and Juliet: Critical Essays*, 73–83, and 'Ideology and the Feud in *Romeo and Juliet*', in *Shakespeare Survey 49* (1996), 87–96; and Watts, *Romeo and Juliet*.

2 On the structure of the play and its use of formal patterning and

parallels, see James Black, 'The Visual Artistry of *Romeo and Juliet*', *Studies in English Literature 1500–1900*, 15 (1975), 245–56; Blakemore Evans (ed.), *Romeo and Juliet*, 6–13; Anthony Brennan, *Shakespeare's Dramatic Structures* (London: Routledge, 1986), 52–69; Nicholas Brooke, *Shakespeare's Early Tragedies* (London, 1968), 81 and 104; Davis, '"Death-Marked Love"', 66; Anthony B. Dawson, *Watching Shakespeare: A Playgoer's Guide* (London: Macmillan, 1988), 139–40; Marjorie Garber, '*Romeo and Juliet*: Patterns and Paradigms', in *The Shakespeare Plays: A Study Guide* (La Jolla: University of California at San Diego, 1979), repr. in Andrews, *Romeo and Juliet: Critical Essays*, 120 and 122; Holding, *Romeo and Juliet*, 17 and 36–7; Stanley Wells (ed.), *Shakespeare: A Bibliographical Guide* (Oxford: Clarendon Press, 1990), 4–5.

3 See Blakemore Evans, *Romeo and Juliet*, 197.

4 For *Romeo and Juliet* as an apprentice piece, see Brooke, *Shakespeare's Early Tragedies*; Charlton, 'Shakespeare's Experimental Tragedy'; Harley Granville-Barker, *Prefaces to Shakespeare: Romeo and Juliet* (1930; London: Batsford, 1982); Avraham Oz, 'What's in a Good Name? The Case of *Romeo and Juliet* as a Bad Tragedy', in Maurice Charney (ed.), *'Bad' Shakespeare: Revaluations of the Shakespeare Canon* (London: Associated University Press, 1988), 133–42; Brian Vickers, *The Artistry of Shakespeare's Prose* (London: Methuen, 1968); and White, 'Romeo and Juliet'. On the play's sophisticated mix of genres, see Susan Snyder's influential account of *Romeo and Juliet* as 'Comedy into Tragedy'; and Brooke, *Shakespeare's Early Tragedies*, 80–106; Kent Cartwright, *Shakespearean Tragedy and its Double: The Rhythms of Audience Response* (University Park, PA: Penn State University Press, 1991), 43–87; François Laroque, 'Tradition and Subversion in *Romeo and Juliet*', in Halio (ed.), *Shakespeare's 'Romeo and Juliet'*; E. Pearlman, 'Shakespeare at Work: *Romeo and Juliet*', in *English Literary Renaissance*, 24:2 (spring 1994), 315–42; Stanley Wells, 'The Challenges of *Romeo and Juliet*', *Shakespeare Survey 49* (1996), 1–14.

5 See for instance Anthony Davies, 'The Film Versions of *Romeo and Juliet*', in *Shakespeare Survey 49* (1996), 153–62; Jack Jorgens, *Shakespeare on Film* (Bloomington, Ind.: Indiana University Press, 1977), repr. in Andrews, *Romeo and Juliet: Critical Essays*, 163–76; Kahn, 'Coming of Age in Verona'; Marianne Novy, 'Violence, Love, and Gender in *Romeo and Juliet* and *Troilus and Cressida*', in *Love's Argument: Relations in Shakespeare* (Chapel Hill, NC: University of Carolina Press, 1984), 87–97; repr. in Andrews, *Romeo and Juliet: Critical Essays*, 359–69; and Snyder, 'Ideology and the Feud in *Romeo and Juliet*', in *Shakespeare Survey 49* (1996), 87–96.

6 Quoted by Ilana Krausman Ben-Amos, *Adolescence and Youth in Early Modern England* (London and New Haven: Yale University Press,

1994), 32.

7 Arthur Brooke, *The Tragicall Historye of Romeus and Juliet* (1562), excerpted in G. Blakemore Evans, *Romeo and Juliet*, 213–14 (emphasis added). On Shakespeare's sources for *Romeo and Juliet*, see Blakemore Evans, *Romeo and Juliet*, 6–13; Geoffrey Bullough, *Narrative and Dramatic Sources of Shakespeare*, vol. 1 (1957); Dickey, *Not Wisely But Too Well*, 102–7; Brian Gibbons (ed.), *Romeo and Juliet*, The Arden Shakespeare, Series 2 (1980; London: Routledge, 1994), 32–41; Charlotte Lennox, *Shakespear Illustrated* (London, 1753); Jill L. Levenson, 'Shakespeare's *Romeo and Juliet*: The Places of Invention', in *Shakespeare Survey 49* (1996), 45–55.

8 Quoted by Joan Larsen Klein (ed.), *Daughters, Wives and Widows: Writing by Men about Women and Marriage in England, 1500–1600* (Urbana, Ill.: University of Illinois Press, 1992), 166.

9 John Bunyan, *Grace Abounding to the Chief of Sinners* (1688), quoted in Ben-Amos, *Adolescence and Youth*, 13.

10 Quoted in Ben-Amos, *Adolescence and Youth*, 14.

11 Andrews, 'Falling in Love', 409.

12 Dawson, *Watching Shakespeare*, 135.

13 Mrs. Elliott, *Shakspeare's Garden of Girls* (London, 1885), repr. in Ann Thompson and Sasha Roberts (eds.), *Women Reading Shakespeare: An Anthology of Criticism* (Manchester: Manchester University Press, 1997), 178.

14 On the couple's immaturity, see Bassnett, 'Wayward Sons and Daughters: *Romeo and Juliet*, *A Midsummer Night's Dream* and *Henry IV, Part 1*', in *Shakespeare: The Elizabethan Plays* (London: Macmillan, 1993), 53–71; Niamh Cusack, 'Juliet in *Romeo and Juliet*', in Russell Jackson and Robert Smallwood (eds.), *Players of Shakespeare 2* (Cambridge: Cambridge University Press, 1988), 121–33; Dickey, *Not Wisely But Too Well*; and Richmond, 'Peter Quince Directs *Romeo and Juliet*'.

15 Quoted in Dickey, *Not Wisely But Too Well*, 116–17.

16 Helen Hackett, '"A Book, and Solitariness": Melancholia, Gender and Literary Subjectivity in Mary Wroth's *Urania*', in *Renaissance Configurations: Voices, Bodies, Spaces, 1580–1690*, ed. Gordon McMullen (forthcoming from Macmillan); see also Snyder, 'Ideology and the Feud', 203; and Julia Schiesari, *The Gendering of Melancholia* (Cambridge: Cambridge University Press, 1992).

17 Brooke, *The Tragicall Historye of Romeus and Juliet* (repr. London: New Shakespeare Society, n.d.), 58.

18 Holderness, *Romeo and Juliet*, 29.

19 Kahn, 'Coming of Age in Verona', 347; on the play's critique of patriarchy, see also Bassnett 'Wayward Sons and Daughters'; Kirby Farrell, 'Love, Death, and Patriarchy in *Romeo and Juliet*', in Norman

N. Holland, Sidney Homan and Bernard J. Paris (eds.), *Shakespeare's Personality* (London: University of California Press, 1989), 86–102; Holderness, *Romeo and Juliet*: Laroque, 'Tradition and Subversion in *Romeo and Juliet*', in Halio, *Shakespeare's 'Romeo and Juliet': Text, Context, and Interpretation*, 18–36; Cedric Watts: 'Sexual Politics', in Cookson and Loughrey, *Romeo and Juliet*, and *Romeo and Juliet*.

20 Davies, 'The Film Versions of *Romeo and Juliet*', 160.

21 Jess Dorynne, 'The Insignificant Mother of Juliet', in *The True Ophelia and Other Studies of Shakespeare's Women By an Actress* (London, 1913), 73. See also Faucit, *On Some of Shakespeare's Female Characters*; and Cusack, 'Juliet in *Romeo and Juliet*'.

22 Faucit, *On Some of Shakespeare's Female Characters*, 112.

23 *The Memoirs of Anne, Lady Halkett, and Ann, Lady Fanshawe*, ed. John Loftis (Oxford: Clarendon, 1979), 141.

24 Davies, 'The Film Versions of *Romeo and Juliet*', 160.

25 Brenda Bruce, 'Nurse in *Romeo and Juliet*' in Philip Brockbank (ed.), *Players of Shakespeare 1* (Cambridge: Cambridge University Press, 1985), 91. See also Kahn, 'Coming of Age in Verona', 348.

26 *http://www.romeoandjuliet.com/players/pn3.html*, p. 5.

27 Quoted in Klein, *Daughters, Wives and Widows*, 17, 22.

28 Wrightson, *English Society 1580–1680*, 92 (emphasis in original).

29 William Perkins, *Christian Economy*, in Klein (ed.), *Daughters, Wives and Widows*, 172.

30 For a brief summary of contemporary theoretical approaches, see Raman Selden, *A Reader's Guide to Contemporary Literary Theory* (London: Harvester Wheatsheaf, 1989), esp. 103–9.

31 Peter J. Smith, *Social Shakespeare: Aspects of Renaissance Dramaturgy and Contemporary Society* (London: Macmillan, 1995), 127–8.

CHAPTER 3. CONSTRUCTING IDENTITIES

1 Marjorie Garber, *Coming of Age in Shakespeare* (London and New York: Methuen, 1981), 163–4.

2 Mikhail Bakhtin, *Rabelais and His World*, trans. Helene Iswolsky (Cambridge, MA: MIT Press, 1968), 320. See also Peter Stallybrass, 'Patriarchal Territories: The Body Enclosed', in Margaret Ferguson, Maureen Quilligan and Nancy Vickers (eds.), *Rewriting the Renaissance: The Discourses of Sexual Difference in Early Modern Europe* (Chicago: Chicago University Press, 1985), 124.

3 Bakhtin, *Rabelais and His World*, 21.

4 On womb/tomb imagery in the play, see Belsey, 'The Name of the Rose in *Romeo and Juliet*', in *Yearbook of English Studies*, 23 (1993), 126–42; Farrell, 'Love, Death and Patriarchy'; Jorgens, *Shakespeare on Film*;

Knowles, 'Carnival and Death in *Romeo and Juliet*: A Bakhtinian Reading', in *Shakespeare Survey 49* (1996), 69–85; Levin, 'Form and Formality in *Romeo and Juliet*', *Shakespeare Quarterly*, 11 (winter 1960), 3–11, repr. in Cole, *Twentieth Century Interpretations of 'Romeo and Juliet'*, 85–95; Ozark Holmer, 'The Poetics of Paradox'; Snow, 'Language and Sexual Difference in *Romeo and Juliet*', in Peter Erickson and Coppelia Kahn (eds.), *Shakespeare's 'Rough Magic': Renaissance Essays in Honor of C. L. Barber* (London: Associated University Press, 1985), 168–92, repr. in Andrews, *Romeo and Juliet: Critical Essays*, 371–401.

5 Holding, *Romeo and Juliet*, 55.

6 Knowles, 'Carnival and Death', 71.

7 Mrs. David Ogilvy, 'Juliet and the Friar', in *The Keepsake 1885*, ed. Miss Power, 74–9 (pp. 74–5).

8 Bulwer Lytton, 'Miss Anderson's Juliet', *Shakespeariana*, 2 (1885), 11–12.

9 Cusack, 'Juliet in *Romeo and Juliet*', 129.

10 Mary Bly, 'Bawdy Puns and Lustful Virgins: The Legacy of Juliet's Desire in Comedies of the Early 1600s', *Shakespeare Survey 49* (1996), 99.

11 Ibid., 105. On Juliet's epithalamion, see also Belsey, 'The Name of the Rose'; Brooke, *Shakespeare's Early Tragedies*; Philip Davis, 'Nineteenth-century Juliet', in *Shakespeare Survey 49* (1996), 131–40; Gibbons, *Romeo and Juliet*; Knowles, 'Carnival and Death'; Kristeva, '*Romeo and Juliet*: Love-Hatred in the Couple', from *Tales of Love*, repr. in John Drakakis (ed.), *Shakespearean Tragedy* (London: Longman, 1992), 296–315; Gary M. McCown, '"Runnawares Eyes" and Juliet's Epithalamium', *Shakespeare Quarterly* 27 (1976), 150–70; Novy, 'Violence, Love, and Gender'; Gayle Whittier, 'The Sonnet's Body and the Body Sonnetized in *Romeo and Juliet*', in *Shakespeare Quarterly* 40:1 (spring 1989), 27–41.

12 Juan Luis Vives, *The Instruction of a Christian Woman*, quoted in Klein, *Daughters, Wives and Widows*, 111.

13 Richard Brathwaite, *The English Gentlewoman*, quoted in Klein, *Daughters, Wives and Widows*, 237.

14 Ibid., 242.

15 See Murray J. Levith, *Shakespeare's Italian Setting and Plays* (Basingstoke: Macmillan, 1989); and Angela Locatelli, 'The Fictional World of *Romeo and Juliet*: Cultural Connotations of an Italian Setting', in Michele Marrapodi, A. J. Hoenselaars, Marcello Cappuzzo, and L. Falson Santucci (eds.), *Shakespeare's Italy: Functions of Italian Locations in Renaissance Drama* (Manchester: Manchester University Press, 1993).

16 Roger Ascham, *The Scholemaster* (1570), quoted in Levith, *Shakespeare's Italian Setting and Plays*, 6.

17 Constance O'Brien (1879), in Thompson and Roberts, *Women Reading*

Shakespeare, 144.

18 On Romeo's effeminacy, see Cartwright, *Shakespearean Tragedy and its Double*; Davies, 'The Film Versions of *Romeo and Juliet*'; Joan Ozark Holmer, ' "Myself condemned and myself excus'd": Tragic Effects in *Romeo and Juliet*', Studies in Philology, 88 (1991), 345–62; Richmond, 'Peter Quince Directs *Romeo and Juliet*'; Snow, 'Language and Sexual Difference'; Watts, *Romeo and Juliet*.

19 Richmond, 'Peter Quince Directs *Romeo and Juliet*', 225. By contrast, William Van Watson perceives a 'homosexual gaze' in Zeffirelli's film; see 'Shakespeare, Zeffirelli, and the Homosexual Gaze', in *Literature Film Quarterly*, 20:4 (1992), 308–25; repr. in Deborah Barker and Ivo Kamps (eds.), *Shakespeare and Gender: A History* (London: Verso, 1995), 235–62.

20 Quoted by Joseph Leach, *Bright Particular Star: The Life and Times of Charlotte Cushman* (London: Yale University Press, 1970), 175.

21 Faucit, in Thompson and Roberts, *Women Reading Shakespeare*, 186.

22 See Andrew Gumbel, 'Restoring a Shrine to Love', *Independent on Sunday*, 14 July 1996, Sunday Review, 40–1.

23 Quoted in Klein, *Daughters, Wives and Widows*, 16 and 22.

24 Kahn, 'Coming of Age in Verona', 338–9. See also Callaghan, 'The Ideology of Romantic Love: The Case of *Romeo and Juliet*', in Dympna C. Callaghan, Lorraine Helms, and Jyotsna Singh (eds.), *The Weyward Sisters: Shakespeare and Feminist Politics* (Oxford: Blackwell, 1994), 59–101'; Davis, ' "Death-Marked Love" '; Novy, 'Violence, Love, and Gender'; Smith, *Social Shakespeare*; and Watson 'Shakespeare, Zeffirelli, and the Homosexual Gaze'.

25 On the large group of terms used by Shakespeare to describe sex that derive from warfare, individual combat, fencing, and jousting, see Eric Partridge, *Shakespeare's Bawdy* (1948; New York: Dutton, 1960; repr. Routledge, 1996), 42.

26 Quoted in Levith, *Shakespeare's Italian Setting and Plays*, 1.

27 On feuding and fencing in the play, see Jill L. Levenson, ' "*Alla stocaddo* carries it away": Codes of Violence in Romeo and Juliet', in Halio (ed.), Shakespeare's '*Romeo and Juliet*', 83–96; Sergio Rossi, 'Duelling in the Italian manner: The case of *Romeo and Juliet*', in Marrapodi *et al.*, *Shakespeare's Italy*: 112–24; Jerzy Limon, 'Rehabilitating Tybalt: A New Interpretation of the Duel Scene in *Romeo and Juliet*', in Halio, Shakespeare's '*Romeo and Juliet*', 97–106; and Joan Ozark Holmer, ' "Draw, if you be men": Saviolo's Significance for *Romeo and Juliet*', Shakespeare Quarterly, 45:2 (summer 1994), 163–189.

28 Ozark Holmer, 'The Poetics of Paradox', 178.

29 Lawrence Stone, *The Crisis of the Aristocracy, 1558–1641* (Oxford: Clarendon Press, 1965), 225–34.

30 Jill L. Levenson, ' "*Alla stoccado* carries it away" ', 86.

31 On homoeroticism and homosexuality in early modern England, see Alan Bray, *Homosexuality in Renaissance England* (London: Gay Men's Press, 1982); Bruce Smith, *Homosexual Desire in Shakespeare's England: A Cultural Poetics* (London: University of Chicago Press, 1991); Jonathan Goldberg, *Sodometries: Renaissance Texts, Modern Sexualities* (Stanford: Stanford University Press, 1992); Jonathan Goldberg (ed.), *Queering the Renaissance* (Durham: Duke University Press, 1994).

32 Roger Allam, 'Mercutio in *Romeo and Juliet*', in Russell Jackson and Robert Smallwood (eds.), *Players of Shakespeare 2* (Cambridge: Cambridge University Press, 1988), 112–14. See also Callaghan, 'The Ideology of Romantic Love'; Holding, *Romeo and Juliet*; and Joseph Porter, *Shakespeare's Mercutio: His History and Drama* (London: University of North Carolina Press, 1988).

33 Allam, 'Mercutio in *Romeo and Juliet*', 115.

34 Porter, *Shakespeare's Mercutio*, 157. For an opposing view, see Blakemore Evans (ed.), *Romeo and Juliet*, 45.

35 Alan Bray, 'Homosexuality and the Signs of Male Friendship in Elizabethan England', *History Workshop Journal*, 29 (spring, 1990) 1–19, 1 and 13.

36 Ibid., 14–15.

37 Bray, *Homosexuality in Renaissance England*, 75.

38 Quoted by Levith, *Shakespeare's Italian Setting and Plays*, 7.

39 Bray 'Homosexuality and the Signs of Male Friendship', 75.

40 Quoted in Laura Levine, *Men in Women's Clothing: Anti-Theatricality and Effeminization, 1579–1642* (Cambridge: Cambridge University Press, 1994), 22.

41 See James Cusick, 'Teacher Turns Back on Romeo's Loving', *Independent*, 20 January 1994, 3.

42 Ralph Berry, *Shakespeare and Social Class* (Atlantic Highlands, NJ, 1988), 42.

43 For analyses of class relations in the play, see Berry, *Shakespeare and Social Class*; Callaghan, 'The Ideology of Romantic Love'; Farrell, 'Love, Death and Patriarchy'; Holderness, *Romeo and Juliet*; Jorgens, *Shakespeare on Film*; Levenson, '"Alla stoccado carries it away"'; Smith, *Social Shakespeare*; Nathanial Wallace, 'Cultural Tropology in *Romeo and Juliet*', *Studies in Philology*, 88 (1991), 329–44.

44 O'Brien, in Thompson and Roberts, *Women Reading Shakespeare*, 143.

45 Faucit, *On Some of Shakespeare's Female Characters*, 115. See also Jameson, *Shakespeare's Heroines*, Vickers, *The Artistry of Shakespeare's Prose*: Watts, *Romeo and Juliet*; and Wells, 'Juliet's Nurse: The Uses of Inconsequentiality', in Philip Edwards *et al.* (eds.), *Shakespeare's Styles* (Cambridge: Cambridge University Press, 1980), repr. in Andrews, *Romeo and Juliet: Critical Essays*, 197–214.

46 Wells, 'Juliet's Nurse', 199–201.

47 See Andreas, 'The Neutering of *Romeo and Juliet*', and Gibson, '"O, what learning is!"'

48 Berry, *Shakespeare and Social Class*, 40.

49 Quoted in Klein, *Daughters, Wives and Widows*, 102.

50 Jameson, *Shakespeare's Heroines*, 95. See also Dawson, *Watching Shakespeare*; and Faucit, *On Some of Shakespeare's Female Characters*.

51 Quoted by Valerie Fildes, *Wet Nursing: A History from Antiquity to the Present* (Oxford: Blackwell, 1988), 94.

52 Faucit, *On Some of Shakespeare's Female Characters*, 133; S. T. Coleridge, 'Romeo and Juliet', in Jonathan Bate (ed.), *The Romantics of Shakespeare* (Harmondsworth: Penguin, 1992), 513–19; Dawson, *Watching Shakespeare*; Granville-Barker, *Prefaces to Shakespeare*.

CHAPTER 4. LANGUAGE AND RITUAL

1 On *Romeo and Juliet's* 'literariness' and use of literary figures, see Ralph Berry, '*Romeo and Juliet*: The Sonnet-World of Verona', in *The Shakespearean Metaphor* (London: Macmillan, 1978), repr. in Andrews, *'Romeo and Juliet: Critical Essays*; James L. Calderwood, '*Romeo and Juliet*: A Formal Dwelling', in *Shakespearean Metadrama* (Minneapolis: University of Minnesota Press, 1971, repr. in Andrews, *Romeo and Juliet: Critical Essays*, 85–117); Davis, '"Death-Marked Love"'; Holderness, *Romeo and Juliet*; Laroque, 'Tradition and Subversion in *Romeo and Juliet*'; Ann Pasternak Slater, 'Petrarchism Come True in *Romeo and Juliet*', in Habicht, Palmer, and Pringle, *Images of Shakespeare* (1988), 129–50; Watts, *Romeo and Juliet*, Stanley Wells, 'The Challenges of *Romeo and Juliet*', *Shakespeare Survey 49* (1996), 1–14; White, 'Romeo and Juliet'; and Whittier, 'The Sonnet's Body and the Body Sonnetized'.

On the use of wordplay and imagery in the play, Andreas, 'The Neutering of *Romeo and Juliet*'; Belsey, 'The Name of the Rose'; W. H. Clemen, *The Development of Shakespeare's Imagery* (1951), excerpted in Douglas Cole, *Twentieth Century Interpretations of 'Romeo and Juliet'* (Englewood Cliff, NJ, 1970), 66–75; Mahood, *Shakespeare's Wordplay* (London: Methuen, 1957); repr. in Andrews, *Romeo and Juliet: Critical Essays*; Moisan, 'Rhetoric and the Rehearsal of Death: The "Lamentations" Scene in *Romeo and Juliet*', *Shakespeare Quarterly*, 34:4 (winter 1983), 389–404; Pasternak Slater, 'Petrarchism Come True in *Romeo and Juliet*'; Caroline F. E. Spurgeon, 'Light Images in *Romeo and Juliet*', in *Shakespeare's Imagery and What It Tells Us* (Cambridge, 1935; repr. in Cole, ed., *Twentieth Century Interpretations of 'Romeo and Juliet'*, 61–5; and Whittier, 'The Sonnet's Body and the Body Sonnetized'.

On rhetoric, formal expression and patterning, see Brooke, *Shakespeare's Early Tragedies*; Clemen, *The Development of Shakespeare's Imagery*; Dawson, *Watching Shakespeare*; S. S. Hussey, *The Literary Language of Shakespeare* (1982; London: Longman, 1992); Levenson, 'Shakespeare's *Romeo and Juliet*', Levin, 'Form and Formality'; Edgar Mertner, '"Conceit brags of his substance, not of ornament": Some Notes on Style in *Romeo and Juliet*', in Bernhard Fabian and Kurt Tetzeli von Rosador (eds.), *Shakespeare: Text, Language, Criticism: Essays in Honor of Marvin Spevack* (New York, 1987), 180–92; Moisan, 'Rhetoric and the Rehearsal of Death'; Pearlman, 'Shakespeare at Work'; Richmond, 'Peter Quince Directs *Romeo and Juliet*', also Snyder, 'Ideology and the Feud in *Romeo and Juliet*'.

On the play's linguistic diversity, distinctions, and disruptions, see Belsey, 'The Name of the Rose'; Blakemore Evans, *Romeo and Juliet*; Bly, 'Bawdy Puns and Lustful Virgins'; Calderwood, '*Romeo and Juliet*'; Clemen, *The Development of Shakespeare's Imagery*; Holding, *Romeo and Juliet*; Hussey, *The Literary Language of Shakespeare*; Jeffrey Rayner Myers, 'Ut Picturae Poemata', in *Renaissance Papers* (1987), 71–94; Snow, 'Language and Sexual Difference'; James Sutherland, 'How the Characters Talk', in James Sutherland and Joel Hurstfield (eds.), *Shakespeare's World* (London, 1964), repr. in Cole, *Twentieth Century Interpretations of 'Romeo and Juliet'*, 76–84; and Watts, 'Sexual Politics', in Cookson and Loughrey, *Romeo and Juliet*, 9–18.

2 On economic imagery in the play, see Brooke, *Shakespeare's Early Tragedies*; Callaghan, 'The Ideology of Romantic Love'; Garber, '*Romeo and Juliet*'; Holderness, *Romeo and Juliet*; Holding, *Romeo and Juliet*; Mahood, *Shakespeare's Wordplay*; Novy, 'Violence, Love, and Gender'; and Wallace, 'Cultural Tropology in *Romeo and Juliet*'.

3 Blakemore Evans, *Romeo and Juliet*, 12. See also Coleridge, 'Romeo and Juliet'; Faucit, *On Some of Shakespeare's Female Characters*; Holding, *Romeo and Juliet*; Knowles, 'Carnival and Death'; and Levin, 'Form and Formality'.

4 For the view that Romeo's love for Juliet is continuous with his love for Rosaline, see Berry, '*Romeo and Juliet*'; Bly, 'Bawdy Puns and Lustful Virgins'; Calderwood, '*Romeo and Juliet*'; Holderness, *Romeo and Juliet*; and Snow, 'Language and Sexual Difference'.

5 Quoted by Watts, *Romeo and Juliet*, p. xxix. Knowles, 'Carnival and Death', and Smith, *Social Shakespeare*, discusses the bawdy 'medlar' reference, while Callaghan, 'The Ideology of Romantic Love', Snow, 'Language and Sexual Difference', and Watts, 'Sexual Politics', consider the commodification of Rosaline by Mercutio.

6 On women's use of the blazon in *Romeo and Juliet*, see especially Whittier, 'The Sonnet's Body'.

7 Holding, *Romeo and Juliet*, 53.

8 Quoted in Klein (ed.), *Daughters, Wives and Widows*, 34 (emphasis added).

9 On the Death-as-Bridegroom motif, see Brooke, *Shakespeare's Early Tragedies*; Garber, '*Romeo and Juliet*'; Holderness, '"My grave is like to be my wedding bed"'; Holding, *Romeo and Juliet*; Knowles, 'Carnival and Death'; Mahood, *Shakespeare's Wordplay*; Moisan, 'Rhetoric and the Rehearsal of Death'; Watts, *Romeo and Juliet*.

10 See Sasha Roberts, 'Lying among the Classics: Ritual and Motif in Elizabethan and Jacobean Beds', in Lucy Gent (ed.), *Albion's Classicism: Visual Culture in England 1560–1660* (London: Yale University Press, 1995), 325–58.

11 *The Diary of Samuel Pepys*, eds. R. Latham and W. Matthews (London: Bell and Sons, 1972), vol. vi, p. 176.

12 George Puttenham, *The Arte of English Poesie* (1589), eds. Gladys Doidge Willcock and Alice Walker (Cambridge: Cambridge University Press, 1970), 50–3.

13 Snyder, 'Ideology and the Feud in *Romeo and Juliet*', 96.

14 Ibid., 96. For sceptical readings of the play's final rituals, see also Bassnett, 'Wayward Sons and Daughters'; Garber, '*Romeo and Juliet*'; Granville-Barker, *Prefaces to Shakespeare*; Barbara Hodgson, 'Absent Bodies, Present Voices: Performance Work and the Close of Romeo and Juliet's Golden Story', in *Theatre Journal*, 41:3 (October 1989), 341–59; Holderness, *Romeo and Juliet*; Moisan, 'Rhetoric and the Rehearsal of Death'; Snyder, 'Ideology and the Feud in *Romeo and Juliet*'; Wallace, 'Cultural Tropology in *Romeo and Juliet*'.

Select Bibliography

EDITIONS OF *ROMEO AND JULIET*

Andrews, John F. (ed.), *Romeo and Juliet*, The Everyman Shakespeare (London: J. M. Dent, 1993). A useful basic edition with helpful easy-to-read textual commentaries, a selection of critical readings, a plot summary, and a short introduction to the play; more adventurous and up-to-date than the New Penguin edition.

Blakemore Evans, G. (ed.), *Romeo and Juliet*, The New Cambridge Shakespeare (1984; Cambridge: Cambridge University Press, 1992). A scholarly edition with a helpful introduction that includes a survey of the play in performance, useful textual commentaries, a concise textual analysis, and an abridged version of Brooke's *Romeus*.

Furness, Henry Howard (ed.), *A New Variorum Edition of Romeo and Juliet* (1871; New York: Dover Publications Inc., 1963). An edition collating eighteenth- and nineteenth-century responses to the play line by line, and a selection of critical readings and sources, including extracts from Garrick's version of the play. A feat of nineteenth-century scholarship.

Gibbons, Brian (ed.), *Romeo and Juliet*, The Arden Shakespeare, Series 2 (1980; London: Routledge, 1994). A scholarly edition with detailed textual commentaries, an abridged version of Brooke's *Romeus*, and an introduction focusing upon textual difficulties and the play's date, sources, and themes.

Watts, Cedric (ed.), *An Excellent Conceited Tragedie of Romeo and Juliet* (First Quarto, 1597), Shakespearean Originals: First Editions (Hemel Hempstead: Prentice Hall/Harvester Wheatsheaf, 1995). A republication of the earliest text of *Romeo and Juliet* (Quarto One of 1597) with basic notes and a helpful introduction.

Brooke's *Romeus and Juliet*

Brooke, Arthur, *The Tragicall Historye of Romeus and Juliet* (1562). Excerpted in G. Blakemore Evans (ed.), *Romeo and Juliet*.

CRITICAL WORKS

Allam, Roger, 'Mercutio in *'Romeo and Juliet'*, in Russell Jackson and Robert Smallwood (eds.), *Players of Shakespeare 2* (Cambridge: Cambridge University Press, 1988), 107–19. An engaging account of Allam's performance as Mercutio in John Caird's 1983–4 RSC production, focusing upon male bonding, sexuality, and misogyny.

Andreas, James, 'The Neutering of *Romeo and Juliet*', in Robert P. Merriz and Nicholas Ranson (eds.), *Ideological Approaches to Shakespeare: The Practice of Theory* (Lampeter: Edwin Mellin Press, 1992), 229–42. An intriguing study of bawdy passages censored in recent North American high-school editions of *Romeo and Juliet*.

Andrews, John F., 'Falling in Love: The Tragedy of *Romeo and Juliet*', in Andrews, *Romeo and Juliet: Critical Essays*, 403–25. Surveys contemporary discussions of Fate and Fortune to argue that for an Elizabethan audience Romeo and Juliet are responsible for their tragic deaths.

Andrews, John F. (ed.), *Romeo and Juliet: Critical Essays* (London: Garland Publishing Inc., 1993). A very useful collection of essays representing a wide range of critical approaches to the play, including more recent work on gender and language.

Bassnett, Susan, 'Wayward Sons and Daughters: *Romeo and Juliet*, *A Midsummer Night's Dream* and *Henry IV, Part 1*', in *Shakespeare: The Elizabethan Plays* (London: Macmillan, 1993), 57–71. A feminist, historicist reading of patriarchy, gender, and powers, focusing on patriarchal authority and the breakdown of the relationship between parents and children.

Belsey, Catherine, 'The Name of the Rose in *Romeo and Juliet*', in *Yearbook of English Studies*, 23 (1993), 126–42. A deconstructionist approach to the play, examining desire, the signifier, and the symbolic order, focusing upon Juliet and the final scene.

Berry, Ralph, '*Romeo and Juliet*: The Sonnet-World of Verona', in *The Shakespearean Metaphor* (London: Macmillan, 1978); repr. in Andrews, *Romeo and Juliet: Critical Essays*, 133–45. A study of Petrarchan and formal modes of language, arguing that the play attacks Romeo's Petrarchism and the use of clichéd language and does not identify with the lovers.

Berry, Ralph, *Shakespeare and Social Class* (Atlantic Highlands, NJ: Humanities Press International Inc., 1988, 38–42). A brief study of class and community in the play.

Black, James, 'The Visual Artistry of *Romeo and Juliet*': Studies in English Literature 1500–1900, 15 (1975), 245–56; repr. in Andrews, *Romeo and Juliet: Critical Essays*, 149–61. An account of how staging visualizes themes and structural parallels in the play.

Bly, Mary, 'Bawdy Puns and Lustful Virgins: The Legacy of Juliet's Desire in Comedies of the Early 1600s', *Shakespeare Survey 49* (1996), 97–109. A study of Juliet's use of bawdy in the play, arguing that Juliet breaches Elizabethan social convention; also examines similar portrayals of desiring, chaste women in contemporary comedies.

Brennan, Anthony, *Shakespeare's Dramatic Structures* (London: Routledge, 1986), 52–69. A survey of structural parallels, contrasts, and echoes in the play.

Brooke, Nicholas, *Shakespeare's Early Tragedies* (London: Methuen & Co. Ltd., 1968), 80–106. Examines the play's shift from comedy to tragedy, formal and ritual patterning, Juliet's frank sexuality, and the Death-as-Bridegroom motif.

Bruce, Brenda, 'Nurse in *Romeo and Juliet*', in Philip Brockbank (ed.), *Players of Shakespeare 1* (Cambridge: Cambridge University Press, 1985), 91–101; repr. in Andrews, *Romeo and Juliet: Critical Essays*, 187–96. An account of Bruce's performance as the Nurse in Ron Daniel's 1980 RSC production.

Bryant, James, 'The Problematic Friar in *Romeo and Juliet*', in *English Studies*, 55 (1974), 340–50; repr. in Andrews *Romeo and Juliet: Critical Essays*, 321–36. Examines anticlerical and anti-Catholic traditions in Elizabethan England, and argues that for a contemporary audience Shakespeare's Friar represents a deceitful, unsympathetic figure.

Calderwood, James L., '*Romeo and Juliet*: A Formal Dwelling', in *Shakespearean Metadrama* (Minneapolis, University of Minnesota Press, 1971); repr. in Andrews, *Romeo and Juliet: Critical Essays*, 85–117. Argues that the play dramatizes a conflict between private and public language, focusing on naming, Romeo's use of Petrarchism, and Juliet's distrust of literary 'form'.

Callaghan, Dympna, C., 'The Ideology of Romantic Love: The Case of *Romeo and Juliet*', in Dympna C. Callaghan, Lorraine Helms, Jyotsna Singh (eds.), *The Weyward Sisters: Shakespeare and Feminist Politics* (Oxford: Blackwell, 1994), 59–101. A feminist, historicist reading of desire and patriarchal law in the play, arguing that *Romeo and Juliet* perpetuated 'socially necessary formations of desire' by consolidating the ideology of romantic love and bourgeois family formation.

Carlise, Carol J., 'Passion Framed by Art: Helen Faucit's Juliet', *Theatre Survey*, 25:2 (November 1984), 177–92. Considers Victorian responses to Shakespeare's heroine by examining Helena Faucit's performance and criticism, focusing upon her portrayal of ecstatic love and gothic horror.

Cartwright, Kent, *Shakespearean Tragedy and its Double: The Rhythms of Audience Response* (University Park, Pa.: Penn State University Press, 1991), 43–87. A consideration of the possibilities of audience response, arguing that the play 'parodies the very romance it endorses' through a juxtaposition of the tragic and the carnivalesque.

Charlton, H. B., 'Shakespeare's Experimental Tragedy, in *Shakespearian Tragedy* (Cambridge: Cambridge University Press, 1948); repr. in Cole, *Twentieth Century Interpretations of 'Romeo and Juliet'*, 1970), 49–60. A study of fate and the feud, arguing that the play represents an unsuccessful experiment in tragic form.

Clemen, W. H., *The Development of Shakespeare's Imagery* (London: Methuen & Co. Ltd., 1951), excerpted in Cole, *Twentieth Century Interpretations of 'Romeo and Juliet'*, 66–75. A brief study of imagery and the lovers' language.

Colaco, Jill, 'The Window Scenes in *Romeo and Juliet* and Folk Songs of the Night Visit', in *Studies in Philology*, 83:2 (spring 1986), 138–157. Argues that the balcony scene and 'aubade' (3.5) have 'folklore origins' in the popular ballad tradition of night visits and dawn partings, usually associated with illicit affairs.

Cole, Douglas (ed.), *Twentieth Century Interpretations of 'Romeo and Juliet'* (Englewood Cliff, NJ: Prentice-Hall Inc., 1970). A collection of essays representing early- to mid-twentieth-century approaches to the play.

Coleridge, 'Romeo and Juliet', in Jonathan Bate (ed.), *The Romantics on Shakespeare* (Harmondsworth: Penguin, 1992), 513–19. A brief account of the play; the volume also includes responses by Schlegel and Hazlitt to *Romeo and Juliet*.

Cookson, Linda, and Bryan Loughrey (eds.), *Romeo and Juliet*, Longman Critical Essays (Harlow: Longman, 1991). A collection of concise, accessibly written essays from a variety of critical perspectives aimed at the schoolteacher/student.

Cusack, Niamh, 'Juliet in *Romeo and Juliet*', in Russell Jackson and Robert Smallwood (eds.), *Players in Shakespeare 2* (Cambridge: Cambridge University Press, 1988), 121–35. An engaging account of Cusack's performance as Juliet in Michael Bogdanov's 1986 RSC production, focusing upon Juliet's childishness, maturity, sensuality, and independence.

Davies, Anthony, 'The Film Versions of *Romeo and Juliet*', in *Shakespeare Survey 49* (1996), 153–62. A survey of film versions of the play from 1936 to 1978 (including Zeffirelli and the BBC television production).

Davis, Lloyd, '"Death-Marked Love": Desire and Presence in *Romeo and Juliet*', in *Shakespeare Survey 49* (1996), 57–67. A study of discourses of desire (especially Platonic, Ovidian, and Petrarchan) and identity in the play, drawing upon psychoanalytic theory.

Davis, Philip, 'Nineteenth-century Juliet', in *Shakespeare Survey 49* (1996), 131–40. A study of nineteenth-century views of Juliet, focusing upon Anna Jameson, Helena Faucit (Lady Martin), and Hazlitt.

Dawson, Anthony B., *Watching Shakespeare: A Playgoers' Guide* (London: Macmillan, 1988). A concise, thought-provoking study of the play in production, focusing upon characterization.

Dessen, Alan C., 'Q1 *Romeo and Juliet* and Elizabethan Theatrical Vocabulary', in Halio, *Shakespeare's 'Romeo and Juliet': Texts, Contexts, and Interpretation*, 107–22. Argues that Q1 is valuable for its 'theatrical vocabulary', focusing upon Q1's detailed stage directions and the implications of the lack of scene division in both Q1 and Q2.

Dickey, Franklin M., *Not Wisely But Too Well: Shakespeare's Love Tragedies* (San Marino, Ca.: Huntington Library, 1957), excerpted in Andrews, *Romeo and Juliet: Critical Essays*, 269–83. Famously argues that the play is a tragedy of character, and Romeo's rashness is responsible for the lovers' deaths.

Dorynne, Jess, 'The Insignificant Mother of Juliet', in *The True Ophelia and Other Studies of Shakespeare's Women By an Actress* (London, 1913), 63–93. Argues that Lady Capulet is 'the strongest character in the play', and speculates her fierce nature arises out of jealousy towards her rival, Lady Montague.

Elliott, Mrs., *Shakspeare's Garden of Girls* (London, 1885), repr. in Thompson and Roberts, *Women Reading Shakespeare: A Critical Anthology 1660–1900*, 176–9. Questions Juliet's sexual precociousness, and attacks the Nurse, Capulet, and Lady Capulet.

Farley-Hills, David, 'The "Bad" Quarto of *Romeo and Juliet*', *Shakespeare Survey 49* (1996), 27–44. A comparison of Q1 and Q2 *Romeo and Juliet*, arguing that Q1 represents an abridged version of the play for performance.

Farrell, Kirby, 'Love, Death, and Patriarchy in *Romeo and Juliet*', in Norman N. Holland, Sidney Homan and Bernard J. Paris (eds.), *Shakespeare's Personality* (London: University of California Press, 1989), 86–102. Uses psychoanalytic theory to argue that patriarchy in the play operates 'as a system of beliefs to control anxiety about death', and that Romeo and Juliet's internalization of patriarchal conflicts leads to their suicide.

Faucit, Helena (Lady Martin), *On Some of Shakespeare's Female Characters* (Edinburgh: Blackwood and Sons, 1885; page refs. are to the 7th edn., 1904). Faucit's book is excerpted in Thompson and Roberts, *Women Reading Shakespeare: A Critical Anthology 1660–1900*. An account of Juliet by one of the nineteenth-century's leading Shakespearean actresses, emphasizing Juliet's purity, maturity, and heroism.

Fowler, James, 'Picturing *Romeo and Juliet*', in *Shakespeare Survey 49*, (1996) 111–29. A survey of illustrations of the play from 1679 to the present day, focusing upon the eighteenth and nineteenth centuries.

Garber, Marjorie, '*Romeo and Juliet*: Patterns and Paradigms', in *The Shakespeare Plays: A Study Guide* (La Jolla: University of California at

San Diego, 1979, repr. in Andrews, *Romeo and Juliet: Critical Essays*, 119–31). A useful study of structural contrasts and patterns in the play, focusing upon conflict, opposition, and Juliet's maturity.

Gibson, Rex, ' "O, what learning is!" Pedagogy and the Afterlife of *Romeo and Juliet*', in *Shakespeare Survey 49* (1996), 141–51. A study of school editions of the play.

Granville-Barker, Harley, *Prefaces to Shakespeare: Romeo and Juliet* (1930; London: Batsford, 1982). A study of the play's action, characterization, staging, and act division, arguing that *Romeo and Juliet* is a straightforward and 'immature' work.

Griffith, Mrs., *The Morality of Shakespeare's Drama Illustrated* (London, 1775, repr. London: Cass and New York: AMS Press, 1971). A didactic reading of the play, arguing that the couple's rash, secret marriage and disobedience of their parents lead to their deaths.

Gurr, Andrew, 'The Date and Expected Venue of *Romeo and Juliet*', in *Shakespeare Survey 49* (1996), 15–25. A scholarly account of the date of the play's composition, performance, and possible Elizabethan staging.

Halio, Jay L. (ed.), *Shakespeare's 'Romeo and Juliet': Texts, Contexts, and Interpretation* (Newark and London: Associated University Press, 1995). A collection of six essays on the play, addressing subversion, sources for the Queen Mab speech, duelling, textual variation.

Halio, Jay L., 'Handy-Dandy: Q1/Q2 *Romeo and Juliet*', in Halio, *Shakespeare's 'Romeo and Juliet': Texts, Contexts, and Interpretation*, 123–50. A comparison of Q1 and Q2, arguing that Q1 does not represent an inferior 'memorial reconstruction' of the play but rather a revision of Q2.

Hodgdon, Barbara, 'Absent Bodies, Present Voices: Performance Work and the Close of Romeo and Juliet's Golden Story', in *Theatre Journal*, 41:3 (October 1989), 341–59; repr. in Andrews, *Romeo and Juliet: Critical Essays*, 243–65. A study of productions of the final scene with a focus on Bogdanov's 1986 RSC production, defending the appropriation of Shakespeare's play-text to address contemporary cultural concerns.

Holderness, Graham, *Romeo and Juliet*, Penguin Critical Studies (Harmondsworth: Penguin, 1990). A helpful introduction to the play, emphasizing alternative readings and the play as a performance text, focusing upon the story and structure of the play, interpretive dilemmas, the use of poetic language, early quartos and Elizabethan staging, and the balcony scene; considerable reference to Zeffirelli's film of 1968.

Holderness, Graham, ' "My grave is like to be my wedding bed": Stage, Text and Performance' in Cookson and Loughrey, *Romeo and Juliet*, 19–28. A brief study of Elizabethan staging, focusing upon scene divisions and the Death-as-Bridegroom motif.

Holding, Peter, *Romeo and Juliet: Text and Performance* (London: Macmillan, 1992). A thought-provoking and accessible study of the play, focusing upon the nature of tragedy, language, imagery, stagecraft, characterization, and the final scene, and concise accounts of the play in production, including Zeffirelli (1961), Terry Hands (RSC: 1973 and 1989) and Michael Bogdanov (RSC: 1986).

Inchbald, Mrs. Elizabeth, *Romeo and Juliet . . . As Performed at the Theatres Royal, Drury Lane and Covent Garden* (London, 1806), part of her series, *The British Theatre*. A censored text of the play, with an introduction focusing on the lovers' sudden passion and Romeo's love for Rosaline.

International Dictionary of Ballet, 2 vols., vol. 1 (London: St James Press, 1993), 1207–14. Concise accounts of *Romeo and Juliet* on the ballet stage.

Jameson, Anna, *Shakespeare's Heroines* (London: George Bell & Sons, 1897), originally published in 1832 as *Characteristics of Women: Moral, Poetical, Historical*. The book is excerpted in Thompson and Roberts, *Women Reading Shakespeare 1660–1900: An Anthology of Criticism*. A popular and influential nineteenth-century study of Shakespeare's female characters, arguing that Juliet is a complex heroine who demonstrates a characterisically 'Southern' European temperament.

Jorgens, Jack, *Shakespeare on Film* (Bloomington, Ind.: Indiana University Press, 1977); repr. in Andrews, *Romeo and Juliet: Critical Essays*, 163–76. A critical account of Zeffirelli's film of 1968, arguing that Zeffirelli simplifies Shakespeare's play.

Kahn, Coppelia, 'Coming of Age in Verona', *Modern Language Studies*, 8:1 (spring 1978), 171–93, repr. in her book *Man's Estate: Male Identity in Shakespeare*, 1981, and in Andrews, *Romeo and Juliet: Critical Essays*, 337–58. A concise, thought-provoking, and influential feminist study of masculinity, femininity, sexuality, the feud, and adolescence in the play.

Kermode, Frank, Introduction to *Romeo and Juliet*, in *The Riverside Shakespeare*, ed. G. Blakemore Evans (London: Houghton Mifflin Co., 1974), 1055–7. A very brief introduction to the play.

Knowles, Ronald, 'Carnival and Death in *Romeo and Juliet*: A Bakhtinian Reading', in *Shakespeare Survey 49* (1996), 69–85. A study of the carnivalesque and grotesque in *Romeo and Juliet* drawing upon the work of Bakhtin, focusing upon the body, the Nurse, bawdy, and the Dance of Death.

Kristeva, Julia, '*Romeo and Juliet*: Love-Hatred in the Couple', from *Tales of Love*, trans. Leon S. Roudiez (1987), repr. in John Drakakis (ed.), *Shakespearean Tragedy* (London: Longman, 1992), 296–315. Psychoanalytic reading of the play which argues for the 'unconscious hatred of the lovers for each other', infantile regression, and the symbolic parting from the mother.

Laroque, François, 'Tradition and Subversion in *Romeo and Juliet*, in Halio, *Shakespeare's 'Romeo and Juliet': Texts, Contexts, and Interpretation*, 18–36. Argues that *Romeo and Juliet* is a subversive, dialectical play, focusing upon bawdy and phallicism, the Nurse, 'artificial' language, and death.

Lennox, Charlotte, *Shakespear Illustrated* (London, 1753). The book is excerpted in Thompson and Roberts, *Women Reading Shakespeare 1660–1900; An Anthology of Criticism*. Attacks Shakespeare's use of sources and the 'absurdity' of his imagination as a playwright, presenting Romeo as 'wild and inconsistent'. One of the earliest published works by a woman on the play.

Levenson, Jill L., *Shakespeare in Performance: Romeo and Juliet* (Manchester: Manchester University Press, 1987). A study of seven productions of the play: the possible 'Elizabethan version' and productions by Garrick, Cushman, Gielgud, Brook, and Franco Zeffirelli.

Levenson, Jill L., 'Changing Images of Romeo and Juliet, Renaissance to Modern', in Werner Habicht, D. J. Palmer, and Roger Pringle (eds.), *Images of Shakespeare* (London: Associated University Press, 1988), 151–62. A concise account of productions of the play 1748–1968.

Levenson, Jill L., ' "*Alla stoccado* carries it away": Codes of Violence in *'Romeo and Juliet'*, in Halio, *Shakespeare's 'Romeo and Juliet': Texts, Contexts, and Interpretation*, 83–96. A study of duelling in the play against the context of street fighting, duelling, fencing, and codes of violence and honour in early modern England.

Levenson, Jill L., 'Shakespeare's *Romeo and Juliet*: The Places of Invention', in *Shakespeare Survey 49* (1996), 45–55. A study of Shakespeare's alterations of his sources for *Romeo and Juliet*, focusing upon style and rhetoric.

Levin, Harry, 'Form and Formality in *Romeo and Juliet*', *Shakespeare Quarterly*, 11 (winter 1960), 3–11; repr. in Cole, *Twentieth Century Interpretations of 'Romeo and Juliet'*, 85–95; and Andrews, *Romeo and Juliet: Critical Essays*. An influential and thoughtful study of different linguistic registers in the play, focusing upon the use of 'artificial language' and the play's formal patterning.

Levith, Murray J., *Shakespeare's Italian Setting and Plays* (Basingstoke, Macmillan, 1989), 54–60. A study of the play's Italian references and anglicization.

Locatelli, Angela, 'The Fictional World of *Romeo and Juliet*: Cultural Connotations of an Italian Setting', in Michele Marrapodi, A. J. Hoenselaars, Marcello Cappuzzo, and L. Falson Santucci (eds.), *Shakespeare's Italy: Functions of Italian Locations in Renaissance Drama* (Manchester: Manchester University Press, 1993), 69–84. Argues that Shakespeare's Verona both represents the exotic 'Other' and is analogous to London.

Luhrmann, Baz, producer of *William Shakespeare's 'Romeo and Juliet'* (1996 film). Information on this film can be found at the website *http://www.romeoandjuliet.com*.

Mahood, Molly M., *Shakespeare's Wordplay* (London: Methuen, 1957); repr. in Andrews, *Romeo and Juliet: Critical Essays*, 56–72. An influential study of puns and quibbles in the play, focusing upon the Death-as-Bridegroom motif, the use of bawdy in 1.1., Petrarchan and anti-Petrarchan imagery, and the language of love.

McCown, Gary M., ' "Runnawares Eyes" and Juliet's Epithalamium', *Shakespeare Quarterly*, 27 (1976), 150–70. A scholarly study of Juliet's epithalamium (3.2.1–31), addressing one of the play's textual cruxes and pointing out Juliet's reversals of the epithalamic tradition and inversion of nuptial images.

Mertner, Edgar, ' "Conceit brags of his substance, not of ornament": Some Notes on Style in *Romeo and Juliet*', in Bernard Fabian and Kurt Tetzeli von Rosador (eds.), *Shakespeare: Text, Language, Criticism: Essays in Honor of Marvin Spevack* (New York: Olms-Weidmann, 1987), 180–92. A concise analysis of rhetoric in the play, focusing upon Juliet's use of language and Elizabethan distinctions between admirable and artificial conceits.

Moisan, Thomas, 'Rhetoric and the Rehearsal of Death: The "Lamentations" Scene in *Romeo and Juliet*', *Shakespeare Quarterly*, 34:4 (winter 1983), 389–404. A study of rhetoric in the lamentations scene (4.5), arguing for the mourners' 'ulterior insincerity' and the scene's lack of 'closure'.

Myers, Jeffrey Rayner, 'Ut Picturae Poemata', in *Renaissance Papers* (1987), 71–94. Argues that *Romeo and Juliet* is constructed as a private sonnet sequence leading to a public epithalamion (a wedding poem).

Novy, Marianne, 'Violence, Love, and Gender in *Romeo and Juliet* and *Troilus and Cressida*', in *Love's Argument: Relations in Shakespeare* (Chapel Hill, NC: University of North Carolina Press, 1984), 87–97; repr. in Andrews, *Romeo and Juliet; Critical Essays*, 359–69. A feminist study of masculinity, power, and gender polarization in the play, arguing that Romeo and Juliet seek to establish a mutual relationship in their own private world.

O'Brien, Constance, 'Shakspere Talks with Uncritical People: Romeo and Juliet', in *The Monthly Packet* (1879), 186–97, repr. in Thompson and Roberts, *Women Reading Shakespeare: A Critical Anthology 1660–1900*, 143–4. A lively reading of the play, questioning Juliet's leading role in the balcony scene and Romeo's unmanly behaviour.

Ostlere, Hilary, 'Endless Love', *Ballet News*, 6:9 (March 1985), 14–17. A concise account of the history of Shakespeare's *Romeo and Juliet* on the ballet stage.

Oz, Avraham, 'What's in a Good Name?' The Case of *Romeo and Juliet* as a Bad Tragedy', in Maurice Charney (ed.), *'Bad' Shakespeare: Revaluations of the Shakespeare Canon* (London: Associated University Press, 1988), 133–42. Argues that the play is a 'melodramatic masterpiece' but fails to meet the expectations of tragedy.

Ozark Holmer, Joan, '"Myself condemned and myself excus'd": Tragic Effects in *Romeo and Juliet*', *Studies in Philology*, 88 (1991), 345–62. A study of tragic effects in the play, arguing that Romeo participates in his own downfall, focusing upon Mercutio and codes of masculinity.

Ozark Holmer, Joan, 'The Poetics of Paradox: Shakespeare's versus Zeffirelli's Cultures of Violence', *Shakespeare Survey 49* (1996), 163–79. A study of Zeffirelli's omissions and alterations to Shakespeare's play, focusing upon Zeffirelli's softening of the lovers' 'violent' behaviour, including Romeo's effeminacy.

Pasternak Slater, Ann, 'Petrarchism Come True in *Romeo and Juliet*', in Werner Habicht, D. J. Palmer and Roger Pringle (eds.), *Images of Shakespeare* (London: Associated University Press, 1988), 129–50. A study of Petrarchism and oxymoron, arguing that the dramatic action of the play 'actualizes' the Petrarchan paradoxes spoken in the play.

Pearlman, E., 'Shakespeare at Work: *Romeo and Juliet*', in *English Literary Renaissance*, 24:2 (spring 1994), 315–42. Argues that Q2 represents Shakespeare's revision of Q1 *Romeo and Juliet*, focusing upon rhetorical language, the Prologue and Chorus, the Musician's scene, and the Queen Mab speech.

Porter, Joseph, *Shakespeare's Mercutio: His History and Drama* (London: University of North Carolina Press, 1988). A study of the 'origins' of Shakespeare's Mercutio in the figure of Mercury, Mercutio's speech acts, phallocentrism, male bonding and homoeroticism, and the stage history of Mercutio.

Richmond, Hugh M., 'Peter Quince Directs *Romeo and Juliet*', in Marvin and Ruth Thompson (eds.), *Shakespeare and the Sense of Performance* (London: Associated University Press, 1989), 219–27. Argues that the play does not idealize romantic love and attacks the 'sentimental misreading' of the play by critics and producers, including Zeffirelli.

Ryan, Kiernan, *Shakespeare* (London: Harvester, 1989), 75–86. A chapter on '*Romeo and Juliet*: The Murdering Word', focuses upon language in the play, attacks psychoanalytic, feminist, and idealist accounts of the play, and takes issue with Dympna Callaghan's work.

Salgado, Gamini (ed.), 'Romeo and Juliet', in *Eyewitnesses of Shakespeare: First Hand Accounts of Performances 1590–1890* (Brighton: Sussex University Press, 1975), 189–202. Contemporary accounts of the play in performance, 1750–1882.

Shakespeare Survey 49, ed. Stanley Wells (Cambridge: Cambridge

University Press, 1996). A special issue on *Romeo and Juliet*.

Smith, Peter J., *Social Shakespeare: Aspects of Renaissance Dramaturgy and Contemporary Society* (London: Macmillan, 1995), 125–35. A short, lively study of language, authority (especially in the figure of Escales), and bawdy in the play.

Snow, Edward, 'Language and Sexual Difference in *Romeo and Juliet*', in Peter Erickson and Coppelia Kahn (eds.), *Shakespeare's 'Rough Magic': Renaissance Essays in Honor of C. L. Barber* (London: Associated University Press, 1985), 168–92; repr. in Andrews, *Romeo and Juliet: Critical Essays*, 371–401. Examines Romeo and Juliet's use of imagery to argue that they have distinct 'modes of desire – one reaching out, the other unfolding'.

Snyder, Susan, '*Romeo and Juliet*: Comedy into Tragedy', *Essays in Criticism*, 20 (1970), 391–402; repr. in Andrews, *Romeo and Juliet: Critical Essays*, 73–83. A study of the 'radical' transition from comedy to tragedy in the play, arguing that *Romeo and Juliet* depends for many of its effects upon the arousal and frustration of expectations derived from comic convention.

Snyder, Susan, 'Ideology and the Feud in *Romeo and Juliet*', in *Shakespeare Survey 49* (1996), 87–96. Examines the feud as an ideological imperative, examining social coercion in the play.

Spurgeon, Caroline, F. E., 'Light Images in *Romeo and Juliet*', in *Shakespeare's Imagery and What It Tells Us* (Cambridge: Cambridge University Press, 1935), repr. in Cole, *Twentieth Century Interpretations of 'Romeo and Juliet'*, 61–5. Argues that the dominating image of the play is light.

Sutherland, James, 'How the Characters Talk', in James Sutherland and Joel Hurstfield (eds.), *Shakespare's World* (London: Edward Arnold, 1964); repr. in Cole, *Twentieth Century Interpretations of 'Romeo and Juliet'*, 76–84. Examines the diversity of voices and linguistic styles in *Romeo and Juliet*, focusing upon the formal and colloquial.

Thomson, Leslie, '"With patient ears attend": *Romeo and Juliet* on the Elizabethan Stage', *Studies in Philology*, xcii 2 (spring 1995), 230–47. An account of the original staging possibilities of the play and the integration of visual and verbal for thematic purposes, particularly the bed as bier.

Urkowitz, Steven, 'Five Women Eleven Ways: Changing Images of Shakespearean Characters in the Earliest Texts', in Werner Habicht, D. J. Palmer, and Roger Pringle (eds.), *Images of Shakespeare* (London and Toronto: University of Delaware Press, 1986), 292–304. Includes a brief but intriguing account of differences between Q1 and Q2's presentation of Lady Capulet and Juliet.

Vickers, Brian, *The Artistry of Shakespeare's Prose* (London: Methuen, 1968). Includes a brief discussion of the 'salacious' use of bawdy in the play.

123

Wallace, Nathanial, 'Cultural Tropology in *Romeo and Juliet*', *Studies in Philology*, 88 (1991), 329–44. Argues that social conflict in the play is rooted in a transition from feudalism to capitalism, enacted through the rhetorical tropes of metonymy and metaphor.

Watson, William Van, 'Shakespeare, Zeffirelli, and the Homosexual Gaze', in *Literature Film Quarterly*, 20:4 (1992), 308–25; repr. in Deborah Barker and Ivo Kamps (eds.), *Shakespeare and Gender: A History* (London: Verso, 1995), 235–62. Addresses phallocentrism, male bonding and homoeroticism in the play and in Zeffirelli's film.

Watts, Cedric, *Romeo and Juliet*, Harvester New Critical Introductions to Shakespeare (London: Harvester, 1991). An introduction to *Romeo and Juliet* briefly examining the play's stage history and critical history; textual problems in the early quartos; Fate, Fortune, and the nature of tragedy; sources and their adaptation; romantic love and bawdy; characterization; and sexual politics.

Watts, Cedric, 'Sexual Politics', in Cookson and Loughrey, *Romeo and Juliet*, 9–18. A brief account of gender relations in the play, arguing that the play has 'feministic' features and endorses romantic love.

Wells, Stanley, 'Juliet's Nurse: The Uses of Inconsequentiality', in Philip Edwards *et al.* (eds.), *Shakespeare's Styles* (Cambridge: Cambridge University Press, 1980); repr. in Andrews, *Romeo and Juliet: Critical Essays*, 197–214. A detailed analysis of the Nurse's use of language.

Wells, Stanley, 'The Challenges of *Romeo and Juliet*', *Shakespeare Survey 49* (1996), 1–14. An account of some of the difficulties presented by the play in performance, focusing upon language and characterization.

Westminster Review xliv:1 (September 1845), 1–78. (Anon.), 'Shakespearean Criticism and Acting: *Romeo and Juliet*'. A study of early nineteenth-century criticism and stage practice attacking popular views of the play, including the work of Anna Jameson and Mrs. Inchbald.

White, R. S., 'Romeo and Juliet', in Stanley Wells (ed.), *Shakespeare: A Bibliographical Guide* (Oxford: Clarendon Press, 1990) 188–200. A brief, helpful account of the play's critical history.

Whittier, Gayle, 'The Sonnet's Body and the Body Sonnetized in *Romeo and Juliet*', in *Shakespeare Quarterly*, 40:1 (spring 1989), 27–41. A feminist, deconstructionist approach to Petrarchism in the play (focusing upon the sonnet and blazon), arguing that the slippage between 'word' and 'flesh' in the play reveals Petrarchism and idealized romance to be tragically fatal.

OTHER WORKS

Adelman, Janet, *Suffocating Mothers: Fantasies of Maternal Origin in*

Shakespeare's Plays, 'Hamlet' to 'The Tempest' (London: Routledge, 1992).

Bakhtin, Mikhail, *Rabelais and His World*, trans. Helene Iswolsky (Cambridge, Mass.: MIT Press, 1968).

Ben-Amos, Ilana Krausman, *Adolescence and Youth in Early Modern England* (London and New Haven: Yale University Press, 1994).

Bray, Alan, *Homosexuality in Renaissance England* (London: Gay Men's Press, 1982).

Bray, Alan, 'Homosexuality and the Signs of Male Friendship in Elizabethan England', *History Workshop Journal*, 29 (spring 1990): 1–19.

Burton, Robert, *The Anatomy of Melancholy* (London, 1621), repr. in 3 vols. by Everyman (London: Dent, 1964).

Cohen, Anthony P., *The Symbolic Construction of Community* (1985; London: Routledge, 1989).

Fildes, Valerie, *Wet Nursing: A History from Antiquity to the Present* (Oxford: Blackwell, 1988).

Heinemann, Margot, 'How Brecht Read Shakespeare', in Jonathan Dollimore and Alan Sinfield (eds.), *Political Shakespeare: New Essays in Cultural Materialism* (Manchester: Manchester University Press, 1985), 231–9.

Hodgkin, Katharine, 'Thomas Whythorne and the Problems of Mastery', in *History Workshop Journal* 29 (spring 1990), 20–41.

Hussey, S. S. *The Literary Language of Shakespeare* (1982; London: Longman, 1992). An overview of Shakespeare's use of language, with a concise introduction to rhetoric.

Klein, Joan Larsen (ed.), *Daughters, Wives and Widows: Writing by Men about Women and Marriage in England, 1500-1640* (Urbana, Ill.: University of Illinois Press, 1992).

Leach, Joseph, *Bright Particular Star: The Life and Times of Charlotte Cushman* (London: Yale University Press, 1970).

McCormick, Thomas, H., 'The Women of Shakespeare' (1892), in Lieut.-Col. Fishwick (ed.), *Shakespearian Addresses Delivered at the Arts Club, Manchester, 1886 to 1912* (London: Sherratt & Hughes, 1912), 67–73.

Partridge, Eric, *Shakespeare's Bawdy* (1948; New York: Dutton, 1960; repr. by Routledge, 1996).

Roberts, Sasha, 'Lying among the Classics: Ritual and Motif in Elizabethan and Jacobean Beds', in Lucy Gent (ed.), *Albion's Classicism: Visual Culture in England 1560–1660* (London: Yale University Press, 1995), 325–58.

Selden, Raman, *A Reader's Guide to Contemporary Literary Theory* (London: Harvester Wheatsheaf, 1989).

Stallybrass, Peter, 'Patriarchal Territories: The Body Enclosed', in Margaret Ferguson, Maureen Quilligan and Nancy Vickers (eds.),

Rewriting the Renaissance: The Discourses of Sexual Difference in Early Modern Europe (Chicago: Chicago University Press, 1985), 123–42.

Stone, Lawrence, *The Family, Sex and Marriage in England, 1570–1700* (Harmondsworth: Penguin, 1977).

Thompson, Ann, and Sasha Roberts (eds.), *Women Reading Shakespeare 1660–1900: An Anthology of Criticsm* (Manchester: Manchester University Press, 1997).

Vickers, Brian, *The Artistry of Shakespeare's Prose* (London: Methuen, 1968).

Wrightson, Keith, *English Society 1580–1680* (London: Hutchinson, 1982).

Ziegler, Georgianna, ' "My Lady's Chamber": Female Space, Female Sexuality in Shakespeare', in *Textual Practice*, 4:1 (spring 1990), 73–90.

Index

Page numbers in *italics* refer to illustrations.

127

*Recent and
Forthcoming Titles
in the
New Series of*

WRITERS AND
THEIR WORK

WRITERS AND THEIR WORK

RECENT & FORTHCOMING TITLES

Title	Author
Peter Ackroyd	*Susana Onega*
Kingsley Amis	*Richard Bradford*
W.H. Auden	*Stan Smith*
Aphra Behn	*Sue Wiseman*
Edward Bond	*Michael Mangan*
Emily Brontë	*Stevie Davies*
A.S. Byatt	*Richard Todd*
Angela Carter	*Lorna Sage*
Geoffrey Chaucer	*Steve Ellis*
Children's Literature	*Kimberley Reynolds*
Caryl Churchill	*Elaine Aston*
John Clare	*John Lucas*
S.T. Coleridge	*Stephen Bygrave*
Joseph Conrad	*Cedric Watts*
Crime Fiction	*Martin Priestman*
John Donne	*Stevie Davis*
George Eliot	*Josephine McDonagh*
English Translators of Homer	*Simeon Underwood*
Henry Fielding	*Jenny Uglow*
Elizabeth Gaskell	*Kate Flint*
William Golding	*Kevin McCarron*
Graham Greene	*Peter Mudford*
Hamlet	*Ann Thompson & Neil Taylor*
Thomas Hardy	*Peter Widdowson*
David Hare	*Jeremy Ridgman*
Tony Harrison	*Joe Kelleher*
William Hazlitt	*J. B. Priestley; R. L. Brett (intro. by Michael Foot)*
Seamus Heaney	*Andrew Murphy*
George Herbert	*T.S. Eliot (intro. by Peter Porter)*
Henry James – The Later Writing	*Barbara Hardy*
James Joyce	*Steven Connor*
Franz Kafka	*Michael Wood*
King Lear	*Terence Hawkes*
Philip Larkin	*Lawrence Lerner*
D.H. Lawrence	*Linda Ruth Williams*
Doris Lessing	*Elizabeth Maslen*
David Lodge	*Bernard Bergonzi*
Christopher Marlowe	*Thomas Healy*
Andrew Marvell	*Annabel Patterson*
Ian McEwan	*Kiernan Ryan*
A Midsummer Night's Dream	*Helen Hackett*
Walter Pater	*Laurel Brake*
Brian Patten	*Linda Cookson*
Sylvia Plath	*Elisabeth Bronfen*
Jean Rhys	*Helen Carr*
Richard II	*Margaret Healy*
Dorothy Richardson	*Carol Watts*
Romeo and Juliet	*Sasha Roberts*
Salman Rushdie	*Damien Grant*
Paul Scott	*Jacqueline Banerjee*
The Sensation Novel	*Lyn Pykett*
Edmund Spenser	*Colin Burrow*
J.R.R. Tolkien	*Charles Moseley*
Leo Tolstoy	*John Bayley*
Angus Wilson	*Peter Conradi*
Virginia Woolf	*Laura Marcus*
Working Class Fiction	*Ian Haywood*
W.B. Yeats	*Edward Larrissy*
Charlotte Yonge	*Alethea Hayter*

TITLES IN PREPARATION

Title	Author
Antony and Cleopatra	Ken Parker
Jane Austen	Meenakshi Mukherjee
Alan Ayckbourn	Michael Holt
J.G. Ballard	Michel Delville
Samuel Beckett	Keir Elam
William Blake	John Beer
Elizabeth Bowen	Maud Ellmann
Charlotte Brontë	Sally Shuttleworth
Caroline Dramatists	Julie Sanders
Daniel Defoe	Jim Rigney
Charles Dickens	Rod Mengham
Carol Ann Duffy	Deryn Rees Jones
E.M. Forster	Nicholas Royle
Brian Friel	Geraldine Higgins
The *Gawain* Poetry	John Burrow
Gothic Literature	Emma Clery
Henry IV	Peter Bogdanov
Henrik Ibsen	Sally Ledger
Geoffrey Hill	Andrew Roberts
Kazuo Ishiguro	Cynthia Wong
Ben Jonson	Anthony Johnson
Julius Caesar	Mary Hamer
John Keats	Kelvin Everest
Rudyard Kipling	Jan Montefiore
Charles and Mary Lamb	Michael Baron
Langland: *Piers Plowman*	Claire Marshall
C.S. Lewis	William Gray
Katherine Mansfield	Helen Haywood
Measure for Measure	Kate Chedgzoy
Vladimir Nabokov	Neil Cornwell
Old English Verse	Graham Holderness
Alexander Pope	Pat Rogers
Dennis Potter	Derek Paget
Lord Rochester	Germaine Greer
Christina Rossetti	Kathryn Burlinson
Mary Shelley	Catherine Sharrock
P.B. Shelley	Paul Hamilton
Stevie Smith	Alison Light
Wole Soyinka	Mpalive Msiska
Laurence Sterne	Manfred Pfister
Tom Stoppard	Nicholas Cadden
The Tempest	Gordon McMullan
Charles Tomlinson	Tim Clark
Anthony Trollope	Andrew Sanders
Derek Walcott	Stewart Brown
John Webster	Thomas Sorge
Mary Wollstonecraft	Jane Moore
Women Romantic Poets	Anne Janowitz
Women Writers of the 17th Century	Ramona Wray
William Wordsworth	Nicholas Roe